NEW SWEDEN ON THE DELAWARE: 1638-1655

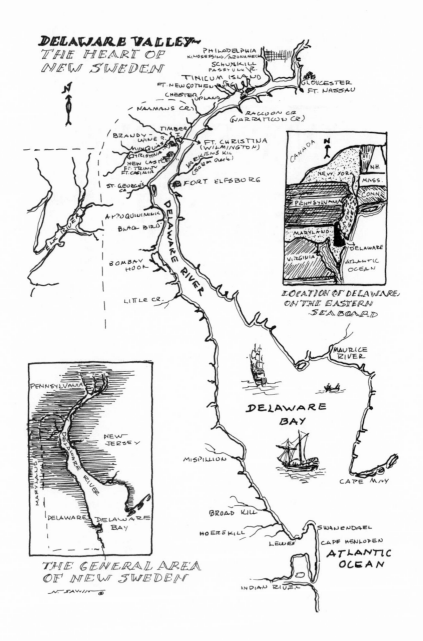

DELAWARE VALLEY—
THE HEART OF NEW SWEDEN

N

PHILADELPHIA
KINGSESSING/PASSYUNK R.
SCHUYLKILL
PASSYUNK R.
TINICUM ISLAND
FT. NEW GOTHENBURG
CHESTER
UPLAND
NAAMANS CR.
RACCOON CR.
(NARRATICON CR.)
BRANDY-
WINE
TIMBER
MINQUAS
CHRISTINA
NEW CASTLE
FT. TRINITY
FT. CASIMIR
ST. GEORGE
CR.
FT. CHRISTINA
(WILMINGTON)
VARKENS KIL
(hog creek)
FORT ELFSBORG
APPOQUINIMINK
BLACK BIRD
BOMBAY
HOOK
LITTLE CR.

ELK RIVER

DELAWARE RIVER

GLOUCESTER
FT. NASSAU

CANADA
N
NEW YORK
VT. N.H.
MASS.
PENNSYLVANIA
CONN.
MARYLAND
DELAWARE
VIRGINIA
ATLANTIC
OCEAN

LOCATION OF DELAWARE ON THE EASTERN SEABOARD

MAURICE
RIVER

DELAWARE BAY

MISPILLION

CAPE MAY

PENNSYLVANIA

DELAWARE RIVER

NEW JERSEY

MARYLAND

DELAWARE
DELAWARE
BAY

THE GENERAL AREA OF NEW SWEDEN

N. SAVIN

BROAD KILL

HOEREKILL

LEWES

SWANENDAEL
CAPE HENLOPEN

ATLANTIC OCEAN

INDIAN RIVER

NEW SWEDEN
ON THE
DELAWARE:
1638-1655
by C. A. Weslager

Kalmar Nyckel
Commemorative
Committee, Inc.

Delaware Heritage
Commission

The Swedish Council
of America

THE MIDDLE ATLANTIC PRESS
Wilmington, Delaware

NEW SWEDEN ON THE DELAWARE

A MIDDLE ATLANTIC PRESS BOOK

First Middle Atlantic Press printing, 1988

ISBN: 0-912608-65-X

The Middle Atlantic Press, Inc.
848 Church Street
Wilmington, Delaware 19899

Distributed by:
National Book Network, Inc.
4720 A Boston Way
Lanham, Maryland 20706

Dedicated to
King Carl XVI Gustaf
and
Queen Silvia
of Sweden

TABLE OF CONTENTS

INTRODUCTION

Where was New Sweden located? This seemingly simple question is not easy to answer because Sweden's American colony had different bounds at different times. In 1638, New Sweden comprised the land Peter Minuit purchased from the Lenape Indians extending from Duck Creek in the present state of Delaware to the Schuylkill River in Pennsylvania. No part of New Jersey was included in this original purchase. In 1640, through additional purchases of land from the Lenape, Peter Hollander Ridder extended the bounds from the Schuylkill north to the Sankikans, and south to Cape Henlopan.

The following year Ridder bought land on the New Jersey side of the Delaware River from Raccoon Creek south to Cape May. Thus the Swedes obtained legal ownership of the tract near present Salem where Governor Johan Printz built Fort Elfsborg in 1643—the first Swedish settlement in New Jersey. In 1649, Printz himself bought land north of Raccoon Creek as far as Mantua Creek, carefully avoiding the territory in the environs of present Gloucester, New Jersey, where the Dutch were occupying Fort Nassau built in 1626. Printz's successor, Governor Johan Rising, further expanded New Sweden in 1655 by buying land from the Minquas Indians stretching to the Elk River in present Maryland. In none of those purchases were specific eastern and western boundary lines named or set down on a surveyor's drawing.

In general terms, therefore, New Sweden at its zenith was an

1

elongated colony that encompassed both sides of the Delaware River and its tributary streams from the capes as far north as Trenton (except for territory in the vicinity of Fort Nassau) without having any stated width.

No state lines existed when New Sweden attained its full size, and Delaware, Maryland, New Jersey, and Pennsylvania became separate colonies, and then separate states, after New Sweden ceased to exist. Local historians quite naturally focus their attention on the events that occurred within the bounds of their respective states. Consequently, the reader learns about New Sweden as it relates to a particular state under study, but not to the Swedish colony as a whole. In the present book New Sweden is discussed from the overview of a contiguous political unit, not from the limited perspective of any one state. The only reason that states are named is to orient the reader to certain places mentioned in the text in terms of modern geography.

Although some of the bounds of New Sweden may be inexact, its short life span was precise; it lasted officially for seventeen years, from 1638 to 1655, when it fell to the Dutch. This by no means implies that all the Swedes and Finns returned to their homeland or that Swedish influence, culture, and language came to an abrupt halt. Quite the contrary, the Scandinavians were unusually prolific, and their children and grandchildren were here to stay, and they exercised their own influence on the successive Dutch and English regimes.

Many events associated with New Sweden actually occurred after New Sweden was a thing of the past, such as the building of Crane Hook Church in Wilmington in 1667. After the political ties with Sweden were broken in 1655, the Swedish Lutherans eventually found themselves without ordained ministers who spoke their language and their only spiritual leaders were lay readers. The fortuitous arrival in 1697 of three Swedish clergymen, Andreas Rudman, Erik Björk, and Jonas Aurén, with the full support of Charles XI of Sweden, gave new life to the Lutherans and subsequently new "Old Swedes" churches were built such as Holy Trinity in Wilmington, Gloria Dei in Philadelphia, and several others. The three Swedish pastors came with William Penn's approval, bearing passports from the King of England, and when they arrived their first obligation was to pay their respects to Pennsylvania's deputy-governor, William Markham. There was no longer any Swedish government in America nor any New Sweden. I stress this because there is a tendency to speak loosely of New Sweden by disregarding its chronology and referring to it as though it continued to exist as a political entity after 1655.

The Kalmar Nyckel Commemorative Committee requested that this book be written in a way "that it will be appropriate to the general public." To me this meant a book written in simple prose, strictly accurate historically, but one in which footnotes would be ambiguous. I'm persuaded that the "general reading public" is not particularly concerned with checking the sources of a historian whose previous writings have been thoroughly documented and that's why I have omitted footnotes. Nor did I think a complete bibliography was necessary in this kind of book; I believed it to be more useful to include a short list of book titles for those who may be stimulated to do further reading.

Dr. Amandus Johnson wrote two hefty volumes containing 879 pages about the Swedish settlements on the Delaware in what was a definitive work when it was published in 1911. If he were alive today many more pages would be required to cover data appearing in books, essays, papers, and Swedish and Dutch translations that have come to light during the last seventy-seven years. To tell the story in a little book like the present one requires digesting and condensing, and laborious rewriting. Wasn't it Woodrow Wilson who wrote to a correspondent, "Please excuse the length of this letter. I didn't have time to write a shorter one." Telling the story of New Sweden with a minimum number of words required omitting some events to permit space for those of greater significance; nevertheless, I have not ignored any of the salient facts in the rise and fall of the colony.

I make reference in the text to seventeenth-century Swedish money, the Riksdaler, Daler, Florin, and Stuiver, but I have found no valid way of equating that specie with the buying power of the inflated American dollar since the two economies were vastly different. I will be a ready listener if and when someone is able to develop a valid standard of comparison. On the other hand, there is no problem contrasting linear measurements: a Swedish foot was equal to 11.65 inches, and the Swedish mile was approximately equivalent to six and one-half American miles. The Swedish calendar also differed from some other calendars in the seventeenth century; Swedes and Englishmen used the Julian calendar, which was ten days earlier than the calendar the Dutch used.

I deeply appreciate the cooperation extended to me by a number of institutions, especially the staffs of the Historical Society of Delaware, the Hockessin Public Library, the Morris Library of the University of Delaware, and the Winterthur Museum Library. I am also very much indebted to the Kalmar Nyckel Commemorative Committee, especially its dedicated president, Camille Julin.

My colleague Peter S. Craig, Esq., provided advice and invaluable assistance in his critical reading of the manuscript. I also thank Dr. Richard H. Hulan for guidance and information. Dr. Barbara E. Benson was an understanding and cooperative editor, and it was her suggestion that prompted the writing of this book in the first place.

It is not by accident that Dr. Nancy Sawin's deft ink sketches and stylistic figures catch the mood of New Sweden and fill the gap left by non-existent photographs and contemporary drawings. She made a special trip to Sweden to authenticate the impressions gained by a careful study of the early documentation. Her drawings emphasize how the vernacular residential and farm structures, household artifacts, canoes, and New Sweden's forts and blockhouses were by-products of logs taken in the Delaware valley woodland.

Others whose assistance is gratefully acknowledged include Peggy A. Tatnall who typed and retyped the manuscript, the Reverend Frank Blomfelt, Professors Stellan Dahlgren and Hans Norman, docents at Uppsala University in Sweden, Lew Grey Squirrel, Tribal Chairman, Nanticoke-Lenni Lenape Indians of

Bridgeton, New Jersey, Dr. Charles T. Gehring of the New York State Library, Joseph G. Lippincott, Malcolm and Marianne Mackenzie, Allen G. Nelson, Lisa A. Nichols, Fred Nicolosi, James A. Rementer, and James A. Schulz.

C. A. W.

PLACES IN THE TEXT

ALTENA, FORT — Name given by Dutch to Fort Christina after Stuyvesant's invasion of New Sweden in 1655.

ARONAMECK — Indian name for a place on the west side of the Schuylkill and also a small stream.

BEVERSREEDE — Fortified trading post on east bank of the Schuylkill built by the Dutch in 1648.

BOMBAY HOOK — English version of the Dutch place-name Boomptjes Hoeck ("Littletree Point") where Delaware Bay ends and Delaware River begins.

CAPE MAY — Known to Swedes as Caput May, a headland in New Jersey at mouth of Delaware Bay.

CASIMIR, FORT — Fortress at present New Castle built by Peter Stuyvesant in 1651.

CHRISTINA, FORT — Swedish fort on present Seventh Street in Wilmington erected by Swedes in 1638.

CHRISTINAHAMN — Village meaning "Christina Harbor" laid out immediately north of Fort Christina during Johan Rising's administration 1654–55.

CRANE HOOK — Known to the Swedes as "Trane Udden," a neck of land between the junction of the Christina River and the Delaware, adjacent to Wilmington Marine Terminal.

ELFSBORG, FORT — Swedish fortress on Delaware River near Salem, New Jersey, erected by Governor Printz in 1643.

HOEREKILL — Dutch name for settlement at present Lewes, Delaware, which means "Harlot's River"; plural, Hoerenkill. Also called Swanendael by the early Dutch, never spelled Zwanendael in contemporary documents.

KAEP DE HINLOOPEN (CAPE HENLOPEN) — Known to Swedes as Caput Hinlopen, a headland in Delaware at the mouth of Delaware Bay.

KAKARIKONG — Indian name for place on east side of Cobbs Creek where Swedes built first water-powered grist mill in New Sweden in 1646; above present Woodland Avenue Bridge in Philadelphia.

KINGSESSING	Indian name for a creek and a place on the creek where the Swedes built a blockhouse called Fort Vasa. Now within west Philadelphia.
MANHATTAN	Island at the mouth of the Hudson River, seat of New Netherland.
MANTES CREEK	Indian name for a New Jersey stream where Mantes Indians lived; probably present-day Mantua Creek.
MARCUS HOOK	Place on the Delaware River in present Delaware County, also known earlier as Marrities Hoeck.
MATINICUM (TINICUM)	Island on the west shore of the Delaware River, south of the mouth of the Schuylkill.
MINQUAS KILL	Name used by Swedes and Dutch for the Christina River, because it was along one of the routes leading to the country of the Minquas Indians, or Susquehannocks.
NARRATICONS CREEK	Indian name for present-day Raccoon Creek in New Jersey, often rendered Narraticon.
NASSAU, FORT	Fortress at Gloucester, New Jersey, erected by Dutch West India Company in 1626; vacated in 1651.

NEW AMSTERDAM	Dutch settlement on Manhattan Island, forerunner of New York City.
NEW GOTHENBURG, FORT	Swedish fort on Tinicum Island built by Governor Printz in 1643.
NEW KORSHOLM, FORT	Swedish fort on west side of the Schuylkill River approximately a mile above the confluence with the Delaware.
NORTH RIVER	Dutch "Noort Revier," used by both Dutch and Swedes in referring to the Hudson River.
PASSYUNK	Indian name for a district on the east side of the Schuylkill River.
PRINTZHOFF	Governor Printz's manse built on Tinicum Island in 1643–44.
SANKIKANS	Indian name for a location on the upper Delaware River near Trenton which was loosely applied to both sides of the river.
SANTHOECK	Earliest Dutch name for New Castle meaning "Sand Point," not "Sand Hook."
SECOND HOOK	A point of land immediately north of present New Castle at or near present Swanwyck.
SOUTH BAY	Dutch "Zuyt-Baye," name for Delaware Bay; also called Godyn's Bay.

SOUTH RIVER

Dutch "Zuydt-Revier," name for Delaware River which Lindeström's Map "A" shows as "Swenskas Revier" ("Swedes River").

SWANENDAEL

Dutch settlement at present Lewes meaning "Valley of Swans."

TIMBER ISLAND

Swedish "Timmer Eylandt" near Fort Christina partially bounded by Brandywine Creek.

TINICUM

Abbreviation for Matinicum; see above.

TREFALDIGHET, FORT

Swedish name given to Fort Casimir by Governor Rising in 1654.

TRINITY, FORT

English translation of Fort Trefaldighet.

UPLAND

Swedish name for present Chester.

VARKENS KILL

Swedish name for Salem River meaning "Hog's Creek."

WATCESSIT

Indian name for place on the Varkens Kill, at or near Salem.

WICACO

Swedish abbreviation of an Indian word Wickquakonick, or Wickquacoingh, applied to a place, later given to a church in Philadelphia.

1. THE BIRTH OF
THE NEW SWEDEN COMPANY

"This place is called Fort Christina Park," I said.

"Why do they call it that?" he asked.

"Because it is named for Queen Christina."

"Who was she?"

"She was the queen of the first Swedes who came here," I answered.

That seemed to satisfy the boy's curiosity. I had taken him to see Wilmington's oldest historical site. After all, a grandfather who has written about Delaware has a duty to try to engender an interest in history in his namesake.

He walked over to the rock outcropping at the river's edge, picked up a small pebble and skipped it across the river. Then he turned and surprised me with a question I did not think he would ask.

"How did they get here?"

I pointed to the monument created by the Swedish sculptor Carl Milles, which was erected as a gift from the Swedish people at the tercentenary celebration in 1938.

"What do you see on top of it?" I asked. He craned his neck as his eyes went up the side of the black granite shaft.

"Looks like a stone boat."

"That's right. It's a small model of the wooden sailing ship that brought the first Swedes across the Atlantic Ocean. It was called the *Kalmar Nyckel*, which means *Key of Kalmar*, named after the Swedish city of Kalmar. It was accompanied by a

11

smaller vessel called the *Fogel Grip,* which means *Bird Griffin*. A griffin was a mythological four-legged animal having an eagle's head and wings and the body of a lion, who guarded the store of gold in a country called Scythia north of ancient Greece. I suppose the Swedes thought that was a good name for a boat, but they usually simplified it to *Grip*. The Swedes came to America on those two ships, and they landed here on these rocks where you are now standing. They bought the land from the Indians and built Fort Christina right here.''

The reference to Indians caught his interest, and he asked me one question after another. ''What happened to the fort? How many Swedes were there? Did the Indians scalp them?''

''That was a *long* time ago,'' I said, ''even *long* before your grandfather was born, and it is a *long* story how the Swedes made the first European settlement here in Wilmington, and there is not enough time today to tell you about it. Now let's go and visit Old Swedes Church. There are some interesting things to see there, too.''

Answers to the questions of why the Swedes came to America and why the two vessels landed at this particular site in the Delaware River valley necessitate turning back the calendar to 1611 A.D., the year Gustavus Adolphus ascended the Swedish throne. His accomplishments as a statesman, an advancer of learning, and a proponent of building Swedish industry were noteworthy, but his fame rests principally on his military leadership. During his reign Sweden became an outstanding military power, without doubt the greatest one in northern Europe.

When Gustavus Adolphus was crowned, Sweden was intermittently at war with three nations: Denmark, Russia, and Poland. He realized he could not do battle with all of them at the same time, so he first took on Denmark, an enemy of long standing. Gustavus Adolphus did not win a resounding victory, nor he did not get everything he was fighting for, yet the Danes were glad to negotiate peace terms with him a year later. That agreement enabled Gustavus Adolphus to withdraw and reassemble his troops, which within two years he led into Russia with the objective of forcing the Russians away from the shores of the

MONUMENT BY CARL MILLES AT FORT CHRISTINA PARK WITH THREE OF THE FIVE LARGE BAS-RELIEFS SCULPTURES AND CAPTIONS BY THE SCULPTOR.

SWEDES BUYING LAND FROM THE INDIANS

RUNAWAY HORSE RETURNED BY INDIANS TO SWEDES

WILLIAM PENN WELCOMED BY THE SWEDES

Baltic. After two years of warfare Russia sued for peace, paying Sweden a substantial indemnity. Then Gustavus Adolphus turned the full strength of his army against the Poles in a war that had religious overtones, because Poland was a Catholic nation, then a natural enemy of Protestant Sweden. Poland also claimed territory on the shores of the Baltic that prevented Gustavus Adolphus from fulfilling his dream of making it a Swedish inland sea. After several victorious expeditions a limited truce was concluded, and Poland ceded valuable territory to Sweden.

During that epoch when a number of wars occurred in Europe, the majority of the people living in northern Germany were Protestants, but their rulers were Catholics who were determined to suppress Protestantism. A religious conflict broke out in the German states, and before it was over other European nations became involved. Gustavus Adolphus, who had his hands full with his own military campaigns and in strengthening Sweden internally, did not immediately take part in the struggle, although his sympathies were with the German people. In 1630, as a champion of Protestantism, he entered what is now called the Thirty Years War (then under way for twelve years) with the best-trained, best-disciplined army in all Europe. The Swedes were victorious in a series of engagements, and in 1631 they defeated the Germans in a major battle at Breitenfeld. The next year in the famous battle at Lützen, a victory that saved Protestantism in Germany, Gustavus Adolphus was killed while leading his cavalry. A combination of personal courage and tactical brilliance made Gustavus Adolphus a great commander. He insisted on going into battle at the head of his troops, not poring over maps and issuing orders from a tent in the rear. His valor robbed Sweden of a great king.

Gustavus Adolphus had no royal sons to succeed him. His only legitimate heir was the Princess Christina, then a child of six years of age—too young to rule as a queen. The government was placed in the hands of a regency of five high noblemen in the kingdom, one of whom was the prime minister, then called a chancellor, Count Axel Oxenstierna. He was an outstanding, honest, sagacious statesman, who was during Christina's minority, in effect, the head of state. One of his responsibilities was to educate the young queen in the ways of politics and diplomacy. She also had tutors for academic subjects and ladies-in-waiting to teach her how a queen should behave. A gifted but unattractive girl, she could read, write, and speak German, French, and Latin fluently at the age of sixteen, and she had a good knowledge of Greek.

Count Oxenstierna's power in the kingdom lasted after Christina reached her eighteenth birthday, at which time her father had preordained that in the event of his sudden death she should take up the crown and scepter. Oxenstierna was deeply devoted to the memory of the king, and in completing the unfinished tasks the king had started, he continued as a prime mover in fulfilling

Gustavus Adolphus's ambition to improve Sweden's position in international trade.

At the time of Gustavus Adolphus's death Sweden had no overseas mercantile activity in America. The spirit of commercial adventure was not present in Scandinavia as it was in England, France, Holland, Portugal, and Spain; military prowess had taken precedence over colonial expansion. There were no Balboas, Ponce de Leons, Coronados, or Pizzaros to pave the way for a Swedish overseas empire and a silver fleet to enrich the kingdom. At the time Gustavus Adolphus was making war in Germany, the English settlement at Jamestown had blossomed into a royal colony; English Puritans had joined the Pilgrims already settled in New England to form a Massachusetts Bay colony; the Dutch were promoting the fur trade with the Indians in New Netherland; and the French were bartering for furs with the Canadian tribes from their citadel at Quebec commanding the Saint Lawrence River. The same year that Gustavus Adolphus's army was decimating German forces at Breitenfeld, Dutch patroons were making a settlement at present Lewes, Delaware, which they called Swanendael.

Gustavus Adolphus was not oblivious to the opportunities for commerce in the New World; he was just too busy with military matters that took higher priority. During a lull in the wars he gave an audience in the fall of 1624 to a Dutch politico-merchant named Willem Usselinx, who had come to Sweden to propose the formation of a company in Sweden patterned after the Dutch West India Company. Usselinx was a founder of the West India Company, one of the most remarkable business organizations ever conceived. The company was owned by private investors but supported by the States General, the parliament of the United Netherlands, who allowed it to fly its own flag and attack and sink Spanish vessels after hijacking their cargoes of silver and gold. The States General gave the company a monopoly to trade along the coasts of North and South America and the western coast of Africa. It was authorized to make treaties with the chiefs of the American Indian tribes. It had the right to establish its own colonies, to set up courts for the

administration of justice, to appoint governors and other officers to supervise its colonies, to build forts, and to hire its own
soldiers and sailors. The settlement and exploitation of the New
Netherland, which included New York, New Jersey, Delaware,
and parts of Pennsylvania and Connecticut, was not an undertaking of the Dutch government but a business venture made by
a company for the benefit of its private investors.

Usselinx maintained that the West India Company failed to
give him the compensation he deserved, so, beset by creditors,
he attempted to organize a competitive company. Not having
sufficient capital of his own, he resolved to try his luck in
Sweden, where Gustavus Adolphus's military successes had
attracted widespread attention. The two men seemed to have
had common interests, and Gustavus approved Usselinx's recommendation of founding a "General Trading Company for
Asia, Africa, America, and Magellanica," also referred to as
"the South Company." The new venture was intended to be a
small Scandinavian version of the West India Company, and
money was subscribed by the king, bishops and other clergy,
high officials such as Oxenstierna, and private persons of afflu-
ence. The pledges seemed to be adequate enough to get started,
but the actual amount paid in was insufficient to meet the
ambitious goals, although some progress was made. Even Gustavus Adolphus, taking off for war again, defaulted on the payment of 450,000 daler owed by the royal treasury.

The "General Trading Company," or, as it was later called,
"the old South Company" encountered some success in minor
enterprises, but it eventually went out of business. Usselinx then
returned to Holland. The desire to form a commercial company
was still alive in Sweden, and with the king's encouragement a
new enterprise called the United South Ship Company was
formed. The investors included the king, the Royal Council,
individual entrepreneurs, and a number of Swedish and Finnish
cities. Assets and some of the vessels of "the old South Company" were turned over to the new company with the consent of
the king and council. The general objective was to build or
acquire sixteen vessels and fit them out for commercial voyages

in European waters, some carrying freight at a fee for private merchants and others for use by the government. One of the cities that subscribed to this venture was Kalmar, and one of the ships purchased for the fleet in 1632 at a cost of 27,098 daler was the armed vessel, the *Kalmar Nyckel*, named after a fortress on an island, "the key" to Kalmar.

The adverse circumstances encountered by the United South Ship Company, and the unsuccessful efforts to form a New South Company, are not relevant to the story of New Sweden and need not detain us. The significant point is that Gustavus Adolphus had nothing to do with the formation of the company that made the first Swedish settlement in America—the New Sweden Company. He was killed at Lützen before it came into existence. Neither did Willem Usselinx have anything to do with the New Sweden Company, which was organized after his return to Holland. But its forerunners were the earlier unsuccessful Swedish companies encouraged and supported by Gustavus Adolphus in his ambition to make Sweden a more important contender in world trade. Needless to say those efforts by the king and his associates led to frustrations and many disappointments. The new company was formed under very unusual and foreboding circumstances. Sweden was without a king, and it was entering a race long underway. Preparations for an expedition to America came at a late date in world history—almost 150 years after Christopher Columbus's discoveries. Rivalry was keen among the European nations claiming lands in America, where they had already planted colonies. A great deal of optimism must have characterized those in Sweden willing to get into this colonial scramble. It might be argued that Sweden had missed her golden moment by spending her strength during years of warfare and that opportunity had passed her by. Chancellor Oxenstierna who had just had his fiftieth birthday did not share that pessimism.

Sweden's land mass was much larger in 1632 than it is today, for it included Finland as well as Estonia, Latvia, and other intervening territory now within the borders of the Soviet Union.

At the time of Gustavus Adolphus's death Sweden controlled the lands bordering the Gulf of Bothnia, the Gulf of Finland, a large part of the northern side of the Baltic, and nearly half of the other side.

Finland had formerly been a country with its own government, but in the Middle Ages it was absorbed by Sweden. As time went on, many Finnish families settled in the north-central parts of Sweden, where the scantily populated forested land was to their liking. Their method of clearing the forests was to burn down the trees and sow grain in the ashes. At first the Swedish government approved of that method but later found it objectionable and declared burning illegal because of the destruction of the forests. The Finns disregarded the laws and continued their practices, which was resented by Swedes who recognized that much of the country's wealth lay in its potential supply of lumber the Finns were destroying.

Another source of wealth in Sweden was natural copper and iron deposits, metals invaluable for manufacturing guns, cannon, swords, and other armaments for use by its armies. Those metals, especially copper, were in demand in other countries, but organized commerce for their exportation lagged far behind the efficient export-import systems in England and the Netherlands.

Despite its large land area Sweden had a small population, which combined with Finland amounted to about one million. Yet the two countries covered territory as large as Missouri, Arkansas, Louisiana, Minnesota, and Mississippi taken together. Less than 15 percent of the population were city dwellers, the vast majority consisting of burghers, miners, peasant farmers, and lumbermen who constituted a combined lower and middle class separated by indefinite economic lines. Above them was the nobility. The burghers, peasant farmers, and lumbermen were not serfs, but hardy, patriotic freemen attached to their Lutheran church. Although many were illiterate, they were skilled craftsmen who made their own wagons, sleds, plows, harrows, household furniture, and domestic utensils. The peasant women, taught from birth to weave, knit, and sew, made cloth and tailored it into clothes and stockings for their families. Their husbands made shoes of leather, wood, or bark, and built their homes of round or hewn logs. Despite a shorter growing season than in the countries of southern Europe, they were able to raise sufficient food to provision their families. There was less poverty in Sweden than in most other European countries.

The Swedes also enjoyed religious freedom, escaping the persecution that drove Pilgrims, Puritans, and Quakers from England to America. Although the Swedes lived under the rule of a king, theirs was a constitutional government, and Gustavus Adolphus "ruled with the aid of the people." Members of the Diet, or Council, represented the peasantry, as well as the nobility, clergy, and burgesses. In retrospect, it is quite evident that if one were to select a country in the early seventeenth century whose people had valid reasons for leaving their homes that Sweden would be low on the scale. That was another reason why colonial expansion did not seem to hold much chance of success. Nevertheless, King Gustavus Adolphus's belated interest in expanding commerce beyond Sweden's shores left a strong posthumous influence on the faithful Oxenstierna, who served the late king for twenty-one years in the interests of Sweden's welfare and glory.

Oxenstierna continued to look beyond the borders of Sweden for economic growth. It seemed to him that every effort should be made to increase exports of Swedish copper. Unfortunately the know-how to penetrate and exploit the foreign market seemed to be lacking, so it was natural to look elsewhere for help. Oxenstierna found that assistance in a prominent Dutch merchant living in Amsterdam, Samuel Blommaert. Although he was a stockholder and a former director in the West India Company, Blommaert, like Usselinx, had sharp differences of opinion with other members of the directorate. He was "disgusted" with the company. He was willing to help the Swedes, not only with advice, but also with his own money. We can be sure he was also thinking of his own interests.

There was nothing unusual about a Dutch merchant offering his help, because Sweden and Holland were then on very friendly terms. Many Dutchmen had come to Sweden to live; some served in the Swedish army; others commanded Swedish ships; Swedish students went to Holland to study commerce, and Amsterdam was recognized among Swedish businessmen as "the best organized commercial city in the world." Oxenstierna was well aware that Sweden had much to learn from Holland, particularly from former executives of the West India Company willing to divulge the company's trade secrets to the Swedes. Communication between Dutchmen and Swedes was facilitated because the Dutch language was widely spoken in Sweden.

Blommaert proposed forming a company to mine and sell copper in the world market, particularly on the Guinea coast of West Africa, where copper was in demand and could be exchanged for gold. While this proposal was under discussion in Stockholm another newcomer appeared on the scene, a friend and ex-colleague of Blommaert's named Peter Minuit. Minuit was not a native Dutchman, but was born of Huguenot parents at Wesel on the Rhine. French by descent, German by birth, he, too, like Usselinx and Blommaert, had been in the service of the West India Company. It was fortuitous that Minuit appeared when Oxenstierna and Blommaert were discussing trade expansion, because he diverted their attention to America. Two other prominent and wealthy residents of Sweden joined the Oxenstierna–Blommaert–Minuit triumverate; namely, Admiral Klas Fleming, a Finn and president of the board of trade, and Baron Peter Spiring, who was born in Holland but ennobled in Sweden under the surname Silferkrona.

Of those five, the most knowledgeable about the New World was Minuit—it was he who proposed founding a New Sweden Company to exploit resources in America. In a letter to Oxenstierna written in Amsterdam on June 15, 1636, Minuit recommended that an initial voyage be made to "the Virginias, New Netherland, and other regions adjacent, *well known to me,* with a very good climate which might be named *Nova Suedia.*" Minuit probably asked himself, why not a *Nova Suedia*? Wasn't there a New England, a New France, a New Spain, and a New Netherland across the Atlantic? In the same letter he specified how large a ship and how many men would be needed; the best season when the ship could sail; and what trade goods were needed to barter with the Indians for beaver pelts and other furs, which he believed offered more lucrative profits than copper. He added that the particular place where he proposed settling was suited for growing tobacco and various grains, also in demand in Europe, and he recommended men should be taken to cultivate the soil. He said he was willing to tender his services to Sweden in the undertaking "which by God's grace, should in a short time result in something great."

Who was this man who confidently offered advice about America, a country that none of the other four had ever seen? Contemporary documents indicate he was then in his middle fifties, an energetic, intelligent merchant-executive with a good education, conversant in Dutch, German, and French, probably also having a smattering of the Swedish language. When he was first employed by the West India Company more than ten years before, he was given the assignment of exploring the Delaware and Hudson River valleys for crystal and mineral deposits in conjunction with a short-lived Dutch settlement made on Burlington Island, New Jersey, in 1624–25. After Manhattan Island was purchased from the Indians, he was promoted to the company's most important American position, director general of the New Netherlands. Minuit was responsible for making Manhattan Island (present New York City) the company's most important settlement, "like a great natural pier ready to receive the commerce of the world." He supervised the development of a profitable fur business with the Indians on the company's behalf, and he laid out a small tobacco plantation at Manhattan and encouraged others to do so to enable the company to meet an ever-increasing demand for tobacco in Europe. The reader will recall that tobacco was a native American plant first taken back to Europe by Columbus, and farmers in Europe did not then know how to grow it.

With his long experience in the Indian trade, Minuit knew which tribes were skilled in hunting and trapping and exactly what kind of merchandise they wanted in exchange for their pelts. Indian preferences changed from beads, bangles, and baubles in favor of duffel cloth, axes, hatchets, mirrors, finger rings, combs, and so forth. Within a few years the Indians also demanded guns and ammunition to replace their spears and bows and arrows. Above all, Minuit was well aware of the company's strengths and weaknesses, its business philosophies and procedures. And, as a company executive, he had access to confidential reports and secret maps not intended to be seen by outsiders. He probably knew more about New Netherland than any other living person; in short, he was an ideal candidate for a competitor to hire.

Minuit had differences with the company's directors over the issue of allowing company executives, called patroons, to start their own private manors in America, a system he favored. His friend Blommaert was one of the absentee-patroons of the Swanendael colony, and as the director-general Minuit officially registered the papers at New Amsterdam for the Swanendael settlement, according to company regulations. However, there was a faction of the directors who objected to patroons establishing colonies. Minuit was caught in the middle.

The differences of opinion resulted in animosities developing both in Holland and in New Netherland. There was bad blood between Minuit and two of his associates on Manhattan Island, who made accusations behind his back. The differences were brought to a head when the directors recalled Minuit and members of his staff to a hearing at the main office in Amsterdam in 1632. Ordering all of them to take the long voyage back to Holland is indicative of the importance the directors attached to the inquest. No record of what went on has survived. After the hearing was over Minuit left the company. It is not known whether he was dismissed or resigned, but if he was dismissed the directors made a grievous mistake in discharging an executive who had information valuable to a competitor.

Resentful of the way he had been treated, Minuit found that his former associate Samuel Blommaert was sympathetic because he, too, was disenchanted with the company's policies. With Blommaert's assistance Minuit offered his services to Sweden. Blommaert recommended him highly, knowing that the Swedes were getting a competent executive. Numerous conferences were held in Amsterdam, Gothenburg, and Stockholm, attended by Blommaert, Minuit, and the Swedish leaders. The discussions were kept secret, because there was general agreement that it would be unwise to let it leak out that Sweden was about to challenge the Dutch West India Company's monopoly in the Delaware valley—the place Minuit had recommended as the site of a potential colony.

A decision was made to send two vessels in the first expedition, the larger of which would carry a disassembled sloop that could be reconstructed when the vessels arrived at their destination and left there permanently. Costs were carefully calculated, and the New Sweden Company was capitalized at 36,000 Florins, equal to 14,400 Riksdaler. Oxenstierna, Fleming, Spiring, and two other Swedes subscribed 18,000 Florins, or one-half the capital needed. Blommaert and five Dutch investors subscribed an equal amount. They agreed to divide the profits, or losses, equally between the two groups. The Swedish government issued a charter authorizing the formation of the New Sweden Company, but it is missing and only some of its provisions are known. The government supplied thirty muskets, a ton and a half of gunpowder, and a large amount of cash as a gesture of cooperation and encouragement, but it was well understood that it was essentially a private venture undertaken by a commercial company.

Although the company's headquarters were in Stockholm, Gothenburg was selected as the port of departure. Supplies and cargo were collected there. Stockholm, Sweden's largest city, had a population of about 40,000, and Gothenburg had about 4,000. Some provisions were obtained in Sweden, but Blommaert bought most of the cargo in Amsterdam, including wines and distilled liquors that he and Minuit knew could be traded in Virginia for tobacco and in the islands of the Caribbean. A large assortment of merchandise was also accumulated for use in the Indian trade, including bolts of colored cloth especially woven to specifications—Minuit knew the color and quality that would have the most appeal to the Indians. Spades, hoes, pickaxes, and other tools needed by the settlers to plant crops were also purchased. None of that activity aroused undue curiosity in Holland because Blommaert had long been engaged in buying and selling. His purchases were not questioned. The fact that the merchandise was shipped to Gothenburg did not cause any stir, because about 50 percent of the vessels then entering the Baltic were sailing under Dutch colors and transporting foreign products.

Experienced sailors were scarce at the time in Sweden, so it was common practice for Swedish skippers to employ Dutch sailors and for Dutch sea captains to command Swedish vessels. Actually, despite the extent of the Swedish seacoast, the country built relatively few ships. In Amsterdam Blommaert hired a number of seamen, who were sent to Gothenburg as the expedition was being organized. The principals offered Minuit command of the expedition, which he accepted. His valuable experience was fully utilized as plans for the expedition took shape in the summer and fall of 1637. There had been general agreement that no women or children should be sent until a suitable site was selected for colonization, a fort built, land plowed, and the seeds taken with the men sowed.

By the end of October the *Kalmar Nyckel* and the *Grip* were ready to sail. They left Gothenburg harbor on a cold day in the beginning of November 1637. The total number of men on the two vessels is not known, but there were probably less than sixty or seventy, equally divided between Swedes and Dutch. The majority of the sailors were Dutch, and the majority of the soldiers were Swedish. Oxenstierna would have preferred a cadre of his own countrymen to be a part of the initial population of New Sweden, but nationality was of lesser importance than establishing a colony that flew the Swedish flag.

Whether there were Finns in the first contingent is not known, because the names of only a few of the men were recorded. Jan Hindricksen van der Water was captain of the *Kalmar Nyckel* and Michel Symonssen was the first mate; both were Dutch. Symonssen had previously sailed in American waters and had some familiarity with the coast of North America. Jacob Evertssen Sandelin, the second mate, was a Scot, one of many footloose sailors from the British Isles who sought their fortunes in maritime Holland. Andrian Joransen was captain of the *Grip,* and the likelihood is that he was Dutch, as was Andres Lucassen, who went as an Indian interpreter having previously been in New Netherland. Johan Jochimssen, a gunner on the *Kalmar Nyckel,* was from Cappel in Schleswig-Holstein, and Peter Johanssen, the upper boatswain, was from Bemster in Holland. Måns Nilsson Kling, in command of the soldiers, was Swedish or Finnish, and Hendrick Huygen, from Wesel on the lower Rhine, a nephew of Minuit's, was the commissary in charge of supplies. Huygen's cousin Gotfried Harmer, a German boy from

Worms, went along with him as a sort of apprentice-servant. Herrman Andersson, Johan Svensson, and Sander Clerck were three of the Swedish sailors, and Klas Jansson was referred to as a "freeman."

There were two barber-surgeons in the crew, Hans Janeke from Konigsberg, Prussia, and Timen Stiddem from Hamel in Sweden.* Barber-surgeons, as the name of their trade implies, cut hair, trimmed beards, and shaved the men. They also rendered dental and medical care such as setting broken bones, amputating wounded or diseased limbs, and prescribing herb cures and other medicaments. They were proficient in bleeding their patients, a common procedure in treating ailments.

The nationalities of the men in the first expedition, and those who later came to New Sweden, cannot be determined by their names. Some Dutchmen bore names that appear to be Swedish, and some Swedish names sound Dutch. Finns usually had Swedish names. Unless there is specific documentary reference to an individual's nationality it is difficult to place the land of his birth.

A long letter containing thirty-two articles was circulated among the skippers, the crews, and the soldiers on both vessels. A copy still exists, and from it we learn that soldiers and sailors alike were instructed to obey their respective commanders and to have their weapons ready for emergencies. Stealing would be severely punished; fighting and drunkenness were strictly prohibited, as was dice throwing and other forms of gambling. Prayers were to be conducted morning and evening, and anyone absent from those services without permission was subject to a fine. Minuit, of course, had a copy of that letter, and doubtless had a hand in composing it. He also had in his possession unpublished maps of the Caribbean Islands and the New Netherland coastal areas that had been made by mariners who had sailed those waters, which the West India Company considered valuable confidential assets. Minuit had access to this information during

---

*Dr. Richard H. Hulan's research corroborates that Stiddem was a member of the first expedition.

his years of service with the West India Company, and he was acquainted with mapmakers and sea captains in Holland, from whom he was able to obtain the latest charts.

The two Swedish vessels ran into devastating winter storms in the North Sea, which resulted in their separation. It had evidently been decided before lifting anchor that they would dock temporarily for fresh water at what was called "the Texel," Holland's most important seaport nearest to Amsterdam. There the two battered vessels met again. After their leaks were caulked and the storm damage repaired, both vessels set sail again on December 31, 1637. The delay was caused not only by making the needed repairs, but also by contrary winds, a factor of critical importance for a crossing of the Atlantic. The absence of winds today does not deter plane, train, or automotive traffic, but without wind a sailing craft was immobilized. This was a costly matter, especially when crews were paid by the day. A becalmed vessel on the high seas had no alternative except to wait for the winds to come up again. Food and fresh water were also consumed by the personnel aboard the vessel while the captain impatiently waited for the wind to blow. The storm damage and the delay at "the Texel" were not anticipated when cost estimates were prepared for the voyage, so before the two vessels left European waters the New Sweden Company had already incurred unexpected expenses.

Minuit engaged a Dutch pilot familiar with Atlantic waters and the North American coast to come aboard the *Kalmar Nyckel* at "the Texel" before the vessels resumed their voyage. The two ships finally reached the Atlantic "with its dead calms and howling tempests" after passing through the English channel, the Swedish flags flying in the wind. Reassuring messages had been sent to Oxenstierna because Minuit had no intention of returning to the home port without completing his mission. It is quite likely that executives in Amsterdam of the West India Company were aware that two Swedish vessels had been repaired in the Dutch port, but we can be sure that they did not know their destination was the Dutch New Netherland.

If the directors of the West India Company had known the

contents of a second document in Minuit's possession—secret instructions given him by Blommaert—they might have tried to deter the two Swedish ships. Those instructions outlined the course the vessels should follow, and in clear detail directed Minuit to sail in waters and trespass on lands that he knew were claimed by the West India Company. There was no question that he was authorized to make a Swedish settlement within the bounds of the New Netherland, which the West India Company considered a private Dutch preserve.

According to the secret instructions, weather permitting, Minuit was told to land first at the "Ille de Sable," present-day Sable Island, located approximately 100 miles off the southeastern coast of Nova Scotia. He was to explore the island, take soundings of the depth of the surrounding water, and ascertain if there was a good harbor for sailing vessels. If the island was not occupied by Europeans, Minuit was supposed to take possession of it, erect a stone monument bearing the Swedish coat of arms, and name it Christina Island. Blommaert and his associates conceived of it as a stopping-off place for ships moving back and forth between the mainland and as a fishing station. The importance the Swedes attached to the island is implicit in their intent to name it in honor of the queen.

Minuit never reached Sable Island. The instructions gave him an alternate route through the Caribbean, which seems to be the one that the weather and winds forced him to follow. No logbooks of the voyage are known to exist, making it impossible to trace the exact route, but sailing in tropical waters and taking advantage of the trade winds was certainly more practical than braving ice and snow in northern waters in January and February.

If he found it necessary to go by the southern route, Minuit was instructed to lose no time in sailing to the South River, as the Dutch then called the river that would later be known as the Delaware. He was cautioned that the voyage should be done secretly "without touching the North River." Such a warning did not require further explanation. Minuit knew that the North River (later called the Hudson) emptied into a large bay at Manhattan Island, the capital of New Netherland. That had been his home for six years while he served as the ranking official of the West India Company in America. Entering those waters would tip off the Dutch of the arrival of two Swedish ships, and Minuit was not yet ready to make his presence known. That would come in due time.

2. THE SWEDES BUILD FORT CHRISTINA

The secret instructions to Peter Minuit were specific about where in the South River he should make a landing—on the Minquas Kill ("the river of the Minquas"), present-day Christina River. That destination had been decided on Minuit's recommendation before the two ships left Sweden.

The Dutch gave the stream its name because it was one of the routes leading to the territory of the Minquas tribe who lived in the Susquehanna River valley. A journey to their land could be made by paddling up the river in a canoe to its headwaters beyond the present-day town of Christiana, possibly as far as Cooch's Bridge. The canoe was then carried over an Indian portage path to the Head of Elk at present-day Elkton, Maryland. From there the canoeist could take to the water again and paddle down the Elk River to the Chesapeake and thence into the bay's many tributaries, including the Susquehanna. Minuit was familiar with that route since he had visited the Minquas Kill before and knew it was a convenient way for the Minquas to bring their furs to the South River to trade.

No one knew better than Minuit that bears, wolves, panthers, wild cats, elk, and deer roamed the forests of what is now Pennsylvania, Delaware, and New Jersey, and that foxes, raccoons, opposums, rabbits, squirrels, and other small animals were also plentiful. Beavers, otters, minks, weasels, and muskrats thrived in countless numbers in the marshes and streams. In his previous position at New Amsterdam he had exported to

Holland hundreds of pelts from animals trapped by the natives in both the Delaware and Susquehanna valleys, as well as from Connecticut and New York. Those skins were in demand for both men's and women's clothing; no fabric could equal the warmth and glistening beauty of natural furs. Fur coats, muffs, wraps, gloves, and fur-trimmed cloth garments were all in vogue in many European countries. The consuming demand in Holland was for beaver pelts because the soft, velvety fur could be felted and used to make the conical, broad-brimmed men's hats so popular in the seventeenth century. The beaver was native to the Delaware River valley, but beaver colonies were more numerous in the Susquehanna drainage system and in the streams in the foothills of the Alleghenies, the hunting and trapping territory of the Minquas, who were also called Susquehannocks.

The two Swedish vessels entered the Delaware Bay (then called the South Bay or Godyn's Bay, after Samuel Godyn, one of Swanendael's leading patroons) and proceeded up the river. It was then early March of 1638, and spring was in the air. What an exciting experience it would have been to share the view from the vessels with the Dutch and Swedish crews. Conditioned to the monotony of blue water and blue sky since lifting anchor at "the Texel" more than two months before, the appearance of the land and trees was a welcome contrast. Trees were nothing new to the Swedes, but to the Dutchmen, who had few trees in their homeland, the scene was almost breath-taking.

The Jersey pines, or pitch pines, on the bayshore and the cypress and cedar filled the air with a fragrance so pungent that an earlier explorer wrote that "a sick person may recover his health through breathing it." The backdrop of oaks, beeches, chestnuts, walnuts, hickories, maples, and ash—just to mention a few of the other—stood straight and tall, their leaves turning green in the spring warmth. What observant Swede or Dutchman would not have recognized the wealth locked up in this seemingly inexhaustible source of lumber suitable for ship's masts, decks, barrel staves, planks, beams, and clapboards? A major navigable river like the Delaware that led to the sea was a highly valuable natural resource in an age when the international movement of goods and people was largely by water. And the trees came almost down to meet the ships. The mouths of many tributaries on both shores permitted deep penetration of the land by small sloops on either side of the main stream. The first waterways seen by the lookouts on the *Grip* and the *Kalmar Nyckel* were later given such names as Indian River, Broadkill, St. Jones, Slaughter Creek, Mispillion, Cedar Creek, Murderkill, Duck Creek, Maurice River, Cohansey Creek, and Salem River.

One of those streams at the mouth of the bay immediately above the sandy promontory then called "Kaep de Hinloopen" was known to Minuit as the Hoerekill ("the Harlot's River"), later to be named Lewes Creek. On its banks the Dutch patroons started the Swanendael colony seven years before, but nothing remained of it. As a result of misunderstandings with a local band of Indians called the Sickoneysincks, the fort and the buildings in the palisaded area were burnt to the ground in a surprise Indian attack. All of the settlers were massacred. Thoughts of this tragedy must have flashed through Minuit's mind as he sailed past the mouth of the Hoerekill, and he must also have been reminded of the Dutch ships that carried earlier explorers and settlers up the identical river where he was bringing a new nation to settle.

Invisible shoals in the South River could rip a hole in the bottom of a sailing craft or cause her to founder in a sandy grave, and the helmsmen went up the river cautiously, the boatswain's mate on the *Kalmar Nyckel* taking soundings to measure the depth of the water. The river could be navigated from the "Kaep de Hinloopen" almost as far north as the rocky "falls" at present-day Trenton, but only an experienced skipper, or one with a pilot who had been there before, would chance running the full navigable limits of the river.

Reaching the mouth of the Minquas Kill, where the Wilmington Marine Terminal is now located but which was then extensive marshlands, the *Grip* probably preceded the *Kalmar Nyckel* into the stream, moving slowly to enable Minuit to designate the particular landing place he was seeking. As the river narrowed he saw the site in a bend on the right bank—an outcrop of

March, 1638 : THE "KALMAR NYCKEL" AND THE "FOGEL GRIP" LAND AT THE ROCKS AT PRESENT DAY WILMINGTON, DELAWARE AFTER MORE THAN A 4-MONTH VOYAGE FROM SWEDEN.

PETER MINUIT IN CHARGE OF THE EXPEDITION BOUGHT THE LAND FROM THE INDIANS AND ERECTED **FORT CHRISTINA** AT THIS SITE. THIS EXPEDITION WAS THE BEGINNING OF **NEW SWEDEN**. THE **KALMAR NYCKEL** MADE TWO OTHER VOYAGES WITH SWEDISH AND FINNISH SETTLERS.

grey-blue granitic rocks, not a boulder like Plymouth Rock or a huge, towering limestone mass like Gibraltar, but a shelf-like projection sloping down from the land. It was like an empty stage waiting for the curtain to go up and the drama to unfold. Having explored this area ten years earlier for minerals and crystals, with instructions to collect "several samples of each mineral that looks promising," Minuit could not have overlooked the unique topographical feature that the Indians knew by two names: Hopokahacking, meaning "place of tobacco pipes," and Pagahacking, "land where it is flat."

The commercial importance of the site was the deep water where ships as large as the *Kalmar Nyckel* could be anchored, the rocky ledge serving as a natural wharf where the ships' cargoes could be unloaded and passengers could walk from ship to shore. A wooden bridge pivoted on the shore could be built to swing to a ship's deck and used as a gangplank without the necessity of going back and forth in small boats to unload the vessel.

There were other reasons why Minuit selected that particular site for the first Swedish settlement in America: he knew the Dutch had never settled on the Minquas Kill, permitting him to claim that the land was unoccupied by Europeans when the Swedish vessels arrived. It didn't seem to concern him that although they had not settled on it, the Dutch were familiar with the Minquas Kill and had already given it a name. Another reason for Minuit's selection had to do with a practical consideration that could not be overlooked; indeed, at the time of his arrival it was of utmost importance. Personnel of the Dutch West India Company were then occupying a fortified trading post called Fort Nassau a few miles away on the east bank of the Delaware River at present-day Gloucester, New Jersey. Minuit himself had a hand in building that post in 1626 as a place for conducting the fur trade with the Indians. Pelts accumulated there were taken to New Amsterdam and combined with pelts from other outlying trading posts for shipment to Holland. Minuit had reason to believe when he arrived in 1638 that since it was spring, a peak period in the fur trade, Fort Nassau would be well garrisoned by soldiers of the West India Company. If his vessels went farther up the Delaware and were observed from Fort Nassau, he feared they might encounter resistance from the Dutch, and he didn't want to take that risk. By tacking into the Minquas Kill and selecting a site two miles within the stream he could establish Swedish ownership and erect a fort before the Dutch knew that there were Swedes in the South River! By the time they objected he would be safely entrenched.

Before setting up the Swedish coat of arms and starting to build the fort that had been planned in Stockholm, Minuit's first task, according to his instructions, was to make sure that no Europeans were living on the Minquas Kill. He was concerned not only with the Dutch, but also with the possibility of an English settlement. If the land was unoccupied he was instructed to request of the natives "that the land be made over to the crown of Sweden, everything in the presence of the officers; and let them, in the interest of trade, subscribe to the purchase of the land in possession of the savages." He was also told to give the Minquas Kill a new name.

The sloop, or "ship's boat," aboard the *Kalmar Nyckel* was removed and assembled and used to sail upstream on the Minquas Kill to explore the surrounding land. The *Kalmar Nyckel* was too large for the task, and Minuit did not want to risk the *Grip* in water that might prove to be too shallow even for a vessel of her size. After several explorations in the sloop Minuit could report that they "neither found nor observed any sign or vestige of Christian people."

Minuit then fired the cannon on the *Kalmar Nyckel*, knowing that the roar would attract the Lenape Indians, the native occupants of the Delaware River valley. We can speculate that there may have been Indian hunters camping in the woods within the earshot of the cannon's reverberations or that there may even have been a small Indian village in the vicinity. Once contact was made, Minuit, through his interpreter, Andres Lucassen, made known that he desired to confer with their chiefs, and as a gesture of friendship distributed gifts to them.

An affidavit signed by four members of the crew of the

Kalmar Nyckel discloses the information that on March 29 five Lenape chiefs boarded the *Kalmar Nyckel* for a conference with Minuit; their names were Mattahorn, Metatsimint, Elupacken, Mahamen, and Chiton. In the presence of the officers in the expedition the chiefs offered to convey to Minuit all the land he needed to start a colony.

There was no haggling over a price because the Lenape concept of land tenure was entirely different from European traditions of land ownership and sale. That difference should be fully understood because it is important to know how the Swedes justified their claim of possession when problems later arose between the Dutch and the Swedes over land ownership. To the Lenape land was like air, sunlight, or the waters of a river—a medium necessary to sustain life. The idea of an individual exclusively owning the soil was as alien to their thinking as owning the air one breathed or the cool water bubbling from a woodland spring. These were the Creator's gift to all men, and the earth itself was the greatest gift of all because it nourished the corn planted by the Indian women as well as provided edible fruits, nuts, and berries.

As a matter of convenience the Lenape recognized certain family hunting territories consisting of parcels of wooded land of various sizes, bounded by streams, trees, or other natural landmarks. Members of a family "owned" the right to hunt, fish, and trap on those plots; others respected that right because they had similar hunting territories. None of those Indian families conceived of land as a personal possession. Land "ownership" meant the right to use the land, to plant on it, to hunt the animals that lived on it, and to build wigwams on it, but not to possess it permanently in the sense that it belonged to one person or family in perpetuity. One might transfer "use" rights to another person, but that did not mean that the "owner" permanently dispossessed himself from the use of the land.

In contrast, land in Europe had been divided and subdivided for so many centuries that the phenomenon of unoccupied land having no owner was inconceivable. The common man in Holland and Sweden lived in a world where all the land belonged to somebody—the government, the church, wealthy landowners, commercial companies, landlords, and, in some instances, the common man may have owned a small plot himself. Real estate was alienable, which simply means an owner could deed it to a new owner. When Minuit in good faith prepared the deeds for the land he wanted to buy from the Indians he was simply following European practice, but that was something the Lenape did not then understand.

The five Lenape chiefs were under the impression they were granting Minuit and his people the right to share the land with them. When they affixed their marks to the deeds they did not know they were transferring permanent ownership to the Swedes. It was not their intent to give up their right to continue to use the land; they meant their action as a genuine gesture of hospitality. Deeply ingrained in Lenape tradition was the obligation they felt to share their food and the comfort of their wigwams with any visitor—white, black, or Indian—who came in peace to their villages. The kind of warm hospitality they extended, which even included sharing the pleasures of a wife or daughter with an overnight guest, was unknown in Europe. In return, a visitor was expected to give presents, not in payment for favors but as a gesture of friendship. Europeans completely misunderstood such hospitality and accused the Indians of prostituting their wives and daughters.

How about the trade goods that Minuit gave to the chiefs, which they received with delight? Did they not accept them as compensation for the land, as Minuit intended? From their viewpoint the chiefs considered the cloth, axes, mirrors, iron pots, and other merchandise, which were products of great value to them, as gifts generously tendered in return for the right to share the land with the Indians, not as reimbursement.

Minuit executed two deeds with the chiefs. The first transferred lands to the Swedes from the Minquas Kill south to Bombay Hook or Duck Creek, a distance of approximately forty miles, and the second, the area north of the Minquas Kill as far as the Schuylkill River, a distance of perhaps twenty-seven miles. The eastern bound was the South River or the Lenape Wihittuck

FIVE INDIAN CHIEFS GREETING MINUIT

METAL AXES GLASS BEADS BOLTS OF CLOTH

TRADING ITEMS GIVEN TO THE INDIANS

LOADING FURS & TOBACCO ON THE KALMAR NYCKEL

("river of the Lenape"), as the Indians called it, but no western
boundary was named. At that time little was known of the land
west of the South River.

After the deeds were signed the cannons on the vessel were
fired again in the Swedish salute of two guns; the coat of arms
of the Queen of Sweden was erected on the shore; and the land
was officially christened New Sweden. Minuit gave the Minquas
Kill a German name, the Elbe River, and the carpenters, assisted
by soldiers and sailors, set about building a fort at "the Rocks."

Dutch, Swedish, and English relations with the Lenape (pronounced Le-náh-pay, not Lenna-pee) are extremely important in
the story of New Sweden, and the cutural differences between
whites and Indians should be understood. The word Lenape was
an Indian word that meant "common people," or as we might
say, "ordinary folk." The Lenape were also known to the
English as Delaware Indians, although this term was never used
by the early Swedes and Dutch. It is derived from Lord de la
Warre, an early governor of the Virginia colony, whose name
was given to the South Bay in his honor by one of his captains.
As time went on the name of the bay was contracted to Delaware, and the English applied the same word to the river
emptying into the bay and the Indian residents. Delaware Indians
and Lenape are synonymous names for the same people. The
early Swedes sometimes called the Lenape the Renappi, because
of the close resemblance to the liquid consonants *l* and *r* as the
Indian word registered on Swedish ears.

How long the Lenape had been living in the Delaware valley
before the white man arrived and where they came from are
questions that cannot be answered with certainty. Informed
anthropologists consider them to be descended from prehistoric
people called Paleo-Indians who came to the North American
continent by crossing a land bridge in the Bering Straits that is
now covered with water. All the American Indian tribes are
believed to be descended from those Paleo-Indians, who came in
a series of migratory waves, although major differences devel-

oped in the language and lifestyles of the various tribes as they
adjusted to their new homes over several thousand years.

The Lenape were not nomadic Indians who wandered here
and there without having a home. In the area that encompassed
New Sweden there may have been twenty-five or more communities occupied by separate bands, each having a distinctive
name. Those communities varied in size, some having seventy-
five or a hundred men, women, and children, and others two
hundred or more. For instance, the Sickoneysincks, who occupied the area between Lewes and Duck Creek were described by
an early Swede as "a powerful nation rich in maize plantations." They were not a separate "nation," but one of the most
populous Lenape bands. The people of Minguannan were a
smaller group having a village by that name on White Clay
Creek. Along the Schuylkill, which the Lenape called the
Manayunk, there were six separate communities, Poaetquessingh,
Pemickpacka, Wickquaquenscke, Wickquakonick, Nittabakonck,
and Passajung. The latter, from which the modern word Passyunk
is derived, was also one of the large communities.

The Mantes lived temporarily along Salem River in New
Jersey; the Sewapoo along Cohansey Creek; the Narraticon on
Raccoon Creek; and the Sankikan in the vicinity of present-day
Trenton. Those names were shown on early maps or cited by
seventeenth-century scribes. In addition, there were other bands
whose names were not recorded but from archeological evidence are known to have existed. Each of the community names
had a meaning in the Lenape dialect but most of the meanings
have been lost. We know that Passajung means "between the
hills," i.e., "in the valley," and Nittabakonck means "a place
that is easy to get to." The meaning of Wickquakonick, one of
the Indian communities near Philadelphia, is not known, but the
Swedes later abbreviated the word to Wicaco and used it as a
name for a church.

Each of those communities was independent of the others,
having its own chiefs and great men who served as councillors
and participated in decision-making. The chiefs did not rule like
kings, and they had no crowns or thrones. They were demo-

cratic leaders who respected the wishes of their followers. The wife of a chief was not a queen in the European sense of a royal family; she worked in the fields, gathered firewood, and took care of her family and household like the other Indian women. There was no great chief who wielded authority over all the Lenape such as that often erroneously attributed to a chief called Tamanend or Tammany. Actually he was the sachem of a Lenape band whose hunting territory lay between Neshaminy Creek in present Bucks County, Pennsylvania, and Pennypack Creek in Philadelphia County. In 1683 he and another chief transferred that land to William Penn for certain European trade goods. He had nothing to do with the lands occupied by other Lenape bands.

Although the Lenape communities were not held together by political ties they all had something in common—they spoke dialects of a native language called Algonkian (sometimes spelled Algonquian) through which they communicated orally. They had no alphabet, no schools, no books, and no system of reading or writing. Knowledge of their language was passed down from one generation to another. Algonkian was only one of many different Indian languages such as Iroquois (which was spoken by the Minquas), Siouan, Muskohegan, and others. The language of one linguistic group was not understood by the others; for example, the Lenape and the Minquas could not talk together without interpreters who knew the other's language. Those linguistic differences were very confusing to the first Europeans who came to America because they expected all Indians to speak the same tongue. Although Minuit's interpreter, Andres Lucassen, could converse in the Lenape dialect, that does not necessarily mean he could understand the Iroquoian dialect spoken by the Minquas.

The Lenape lived in bark huts, or wigwams, usually built along the banks of a navigable river or stream. There were no streets, no public square, no courthouse or jail, and no police officers. Usually a wigwam was occupied by a single family, but some of the larger ones housed several families generally related on the mother's side. Lenape society was matrilineal, which means that descent was traced through the mother's lineage. A chief's son did not inherit the office, but the eligible candidates were the chief's brother, the son of one of his sisters, or the son of a sister's daughter. The community selected their chief from among the candidates eligible by birth, and sometimes an elderly chief made his preference known before his death. It may seem curious that the lines of descent were traced through the mother, but it made good sense to the Lenape. A mother was certain of the offspring she bore, but a child could never be positive about the identity of his father.

The Swede who visited a Lenape village for the first time must have found the Indian way of life strangely primitive. His greatest surprise would have been the complete absence of guns and ammunition, swords, steel knives, iron hoes and axes, copper pots, pewter and China dishes, and the other metal tools and domestic utensils commonly used in Sweden. The native artifacts were fashioned from stone, bone, wood, shell, and clay. The principal weapon was a bow made of pliable wood fitted with a bowstring of a twisted thong of deerskin. The arrows were reeds tipped with sharp points of flint, chalcedony, jasper, quartz, or deer antler. There were no wheeled vehicles; no horses; no cotton, wool, silk, or any kind of woven cloth; no glass; no precious stones or gold and silver jewelry.

The Lenape women made pots of common clay and cooked their soups and stews over an open wood fire, the pots held upright by supporting stones. Their tableware consisted of wooden bowls, clam-shell spoons, and flint knives—they did not have forks, although meat and fowl were sometimes skewered on sticks held over the embers. In the absence of salt, pepper, and condiments, some of the cooked food tasted flat to a European. Of course, the family gathered berries, nuts, wild fruits, and edible roots in baskets woven by the women, and there were many species of edible fish in the streams like the Minquas Kill, where the shad came to spawn. The Lenape did not make canoes of birchbark like many northern tribes; their canoes were "dugouts"—logs hollowed out to accommodate the paddlers.

They were not as graceful as bark canoes but were sturdy and serviceable.

At certain times of the year the men left their villages to go on hunting trips or to the bay shore to gather oysters and other shellfish. When they took their families with them their home villages were temporarily deserted, which caused the whites to believe that the Indians had permanently vacated, but this was not the case. Raising corn, beans, pumpkins, squashes, and other garden products necessitated remaining at a fixed location during the planting season, and at harvest time the families had to return home again.

Maize, or corn, the mainstay in the Lenape diet, was strictly an American product, which, like tobacco, the earliest Europeans had never seen before. The Lenape prepared it in many ways: corn on the cob was roasted in hot ashes; it was also boiled in clay pots. The corn kernels removed from the cob were mixed with beans to make succotash or boiled to make hominy or a nourishing mush. The kernels were also pounded into cornmeal in a log mortar with a stone pestle. When mixed with water, cornmeal formed a dough that could be molded into ash cakes—small patties baked on a flat stone tilted toward the fire. Dried berries or nuts were sometimes mixed with the dough, and cornmeal stew was cooked with fish and venison. The Indians taught the Swedes many of those corn recipes, and corn pone became a staple food.

The white-tailed Virginia deer, which were abundant in New Sweden, was not only a source of venison, but its antlers and bones were used for tools and its sinews and gut for bindings and glue. The deer scapula (shoulder blade) made a serviceable hoe when fastened to a stick. An important use of deerskin was for making the loincloths worn by the Lenape men, the short skirts worn by the women, and the moccasins which they both wore.

Men and women went topless in the summer, but during the winter they wore deerskin leggings and robes of bearskin to cover the upper parts of their bodies. Lenape men did not wear ornate feather war bonnets like those made by the Indians of the

Great Plains. Young men plucked the hair from their heads with clam shells used as tweezers, leaving a small tuft in the center to which they fastened a feather or two; older men like the five chiefs who came aboard the *Kalmar Nyckel* allowed their hair to grow long. For ornamentation both men and women wore stone or shell pendants around their necks and earrings of animal teeth and claws. They decorated their bodies with tattoos by puncturing the skin and rubbing powdered bark or clay pigment into the abrasions. For their ceremonial dances the men painted their faces and other parts of their bodies with charcoal, vegetable dyes, red ochre, and other colored clays. Women also painted their faces for certain festivities and dances, often daubing a red circular spot on each cheek and reddening their eyelids and outlining the rims of their ears in red paint. This was part of getting "dressed up" for their ceremonies, but when Indian braves went to war they painted their faces with hideous designs intended to make them appear ferocious to the enemy. The Indian skin color was brownish or coppery, not red; the term "red skins," or *peaux rouge*, originated with French explorers when they first encountered northern Indians who applied red paint to their faces.

The Lenape did not coin any money, and at the time of Minuit's arrival Dutch and Swedish currency did not have any value to them. They had no banks where they could invest money and no stores where they could spend it; the accumulation of wealth or worldly goods was not a trait in native tradition. Theirs was not a competitive society where an individual was intent upon amassing more goods than another, rather they were taught to share what they had with others.

Shell beads of several types were a form of "wealth" to the Lenape, but not in the sense of a medium of exchange like modern specie. The Algonkian word wampumpeake meant "a string of white beads" and was shortened by the English to wampum or peake. Dutch and Swedes generally referred to wampum by another Indian word, sewant, (meaning "scattered"), and there were two colors, white and purple. The dark beads were considered twice as valuable as the white ones.

The Lenape exchanged strings of beads, or loose beads, to solemnize or purify transactions from latent evil forces or to seal bargains. As they entered into negotiations with Europeans, strings of wampum beads sewn together to form belts, many bearing designs in the beadwork, were exchanged as a record of the transaction and a token of peace and trust. Beads also had significant uses within the tribe. For instance, if a young man decided he wanted a certain girl as his wife he might present strings of wampum gifts, along with other gifts, to the girl's parents, usually through a female intermediary. If the gifts were accepted, it meant that the girl and her parents consented to the marriage; if the presents were rejected, the answer was no. There was no courtship period nor a wedding ceremony with rings and vows. Following a short waiting period after the beads and other gifts were accepted, the bride's mother or a female relative dressed her in new clothing, fixed her hair, painted her face attractively, and brought her to the groom's wigwam to live with him. There were no formal divorces. If a couple decided to separate, one of them simply left the wigwam and didn't come back. If there were children, they always remained with the mother. Usually the marriage lasted because the division of labor in the tribe required each to perform tasks necessary to the family's survival.

Men hunted, fished, made the weapons and stone tools, built the wigwams, and were the protectors of their families against enemies or predatory animals. Women did the planting and harvesting, tended the fires, did all the household tasks, and cared for the children. Mothers taught basketry, pottery-making, and other crafts to their daughters; boys learned from their fathers. Both had a great deal to learn before reaching a marriageable age, because nature, at times friendly but also unfriendly, was the moving force in their world. Prior to making contact with Europeans the Indians were the providers of everything they used or consumed in their daily life with the possible exception of certain magic cures, medicines concocted by their shaman to treat serious illness. All Indians had to learn to prepare herb remedies to relieve temporary aches and pains and minor ailments. The roots, leaves, barks, stalks, seeds, and flowers growing wild in the woods constituted their pharmaceuticals, and they learned to distinguish the beneficial plants from the noxious ones.

Although money had no utilitarian value to the Lenape during the period of initial contact with the Swedes and Dutch, the Indians quickly developed what almost amounted to an obsession for what they considered the wonderful goods brought by the white man. Who can blame them? They were unable to produce the kinds of tools, implements, utensils, and ornaments like those Minuit brought with him on the *Kalmar Nyckel*. To a Swede a string of glass beads, a pair of scissors, or a brass finger ring represented small monetary value, but to the natives these were rarities of inestimable value that the most skilled native craftsman could not duplicate. What Indian would be satisfied with a stone axe or a flint knife after using the white man's metal tools with their sharply-honed blades?

Once a Lenape squaw cooked in an unbreakable iron or copper pot she was no longer content to use a friable clay vessel that took hours to make and would shatter if it fell to the ground. Imagine her delight with the soft flexible woven cloth that did not have to be scraped to remove the flesh or stretched on a rack and softened by rubbing animal brains into the skin. It could be cut with scissors and sewed with needles and thread obtained from the whites—and Minuit had more than 2,000 yards of such cloth along with the other trade goods on the *Kalmar Nyckel*. Delighted with the woven cloth, an Indian woman wrapped it around her body to form not just a skirt but her first primitive dress. She used it as a blanket to cover her children at night, and her husband found cloth less cumbersome than a bearskin to cover his body in winter and in the warmer months a smaller piece fastened to a deerskin belt made an excellent breach clout.

In adapting to European products the Lenape also developed a taste for alcoholic beverages previously unknown to them. "They drank nothing but pure water," one Swede wrote, but with the coming of the white man rum and whiskey became a curse to the Indians. The European did not realize the consequences of introducing strong drink to a people who had never tasted alcohol before and had no tolerance for it. Little did they realize that not only would liquor set the Indian's head whirling, it would release his inhibitions with unpredictable results. Social drinking in moderation or lifting a glass to cement bonds of friendship were never properly taught the Indians. The Indian enjoyed the sensation of excitement, the emotional release, and then the numbness that resulted from overindulgence. The Indian was not only willing, but anxious to try it over and over again. Liquor became a commodity in wide demand and one for which the natives would readily trade animal pelts or anything else, and it contributed to debasing European-Indian relations. Within a few years acute alcoholism became a severe problem, and like the contagious diseases brought from Europe, especially small pox, it killed thousands of the Lenape.

Since some European pastors who came to America in the seventeenth century, including those from Sweden, were intent on converting the heathen "savages" or "wildlings," as they termed the Indians, a few words about Lenape religion are in order. The earliest instructions issued by the Dutch West India Company to the colonists who settled on Burlington Island stated, "They shall within their territory practice no other form of divine worship than that of the Reformed religion as at present practiced here in this country and thus by their Christian life and conduct, seek to draw the Indians and other blind people to the knowledge of God and his word. . . ." By "God and his word" they meant the Dutch Reformed church, whereas Lord Baltimore was thinking of Catholicism when he instructed his brother Leonard Calvert that his first endeavor should be "the conversion of the savages to Christianity. . . ." To the Swedes the Lutheran church was the only true religion, and the other sects and religious groups felt the same way about their denominations. The Indians were often confused by the diversity of those religious beliefs.

The urge to spread Christianity to the American Indians was a by-product of the religious fervor in Europe that drove Gustavus

Adolphus to kill Catholics in Germany and made martyrs of Jesuit priests in Canada. So far as the Lenape are concerned no serious attempts were ever made in the seventeenth century to understand their religious beliefs. The principal motivation was that they were heathens in need of conversion. We now know that the Lenape believed in the existence of a Creator who made the world, sun, moon, stars, plants, trees, and animals. To them the Creator was represented by indwelling spirit forces present in all natural things, and in their religious ceremonies they paid homage to the Creator and those subordinate forces. They also believed in life after death. They did not worship idols, and, although Swedish and Dutch missionaries considered them pagans, they believed in a God who was everything and everything was God.

The fort Minuit and his men built at "the Rocks" was made of log palisades sharpened at their tops and set together vertically in the form of a square. Four acute-angled bastions projected diagonally from the four corners, three of which were mounted with cannon. Except on the northeast side, the site was flanked by tidal marshes that provided natural protection. Entrance by land was from the northeast, probably via a narrow path that ran into the woods. The main gate opened up on the rocky wharf running down to the river where the vessels were anchored. Two log houses were erected in the enclosure surrounded by the palisades, one a sort of barracks for the men stationed in the fort, and the other a storehouse for food, supplies, and merchandise intended for the Indian trade. Minuit purchased a supply of bricks in Gothenburg before he sailed, and they were probably used to construct a fireplace and oven. Rough benches, chairs, tables, and bunks were probably made of hand-sawed lumber.

Minuit's instructions did not stipulate the name to be given to the structure; in fact, he was simply told to build "a lodge or house in which the people may dwell who remain there close to the sloop." Since Minuit had not landed at Sable Island, he decided that the Queen's name should be used here instead, and he called the post "Fort Christina" in honor of the twelve-year-old girl who had not yet ascended to the Swedish throne. It was at a later date that the stream became known as the Christina River—Minuit had nothing to do with that. His choice, the Elbe River, never clung to the waterway; throughout the life of New Sweden it continued to be called the Minquas Kill by Swedes, Finns, Dutch, and English alike.

It was only a matter of time before the Dutch at Fort Nassau learned that there were Swedish intruders on the Minquas Kill. In mid-April the officer in charge of Fort Nassau protested the settlement. Minuit blithely answered that "his Queen" had as much right in the South River as the West India Company, which was stretching the truth. Minuit learned that his soldiers outnumbered the men in the garrison at Fort Nassau, and there was nothing the commandant could do but notify Director-General William Kieft, who held the same executive post at New Amsterdam that Minuit had previously occupied.

When Kieft received the unwelcome news he sent a special messenger with a letter addressed to Minuit in which he said that Minuit was well aware that the South River had long been in Dutch possession having been "sealed with our blood." By that he was referring to the ill-fated colony at Swanendael. He warned Minuit that if he continued with the erection of a fort, attempted to cultivate the soil, and engaged in the fur trade with the Indians "we shall maintain our jurisdiction in such manner as we shall deem most expedient."

This European diplomatic language in the American wilderness didn't faze Minuit, because by the time he received the letter the fort was well on the way to completion, and he had already sent the sloop up the Delaware to trade with the Indians. He offered more goods for their beaver pelts than the Dutch were paying in an attempt to corner the market. Minuit ignored Kieft's warning because he knew Kieft would not take up arms on his own initiative against a fort flying the flag of a friendly nation. Minuit's strategy was to establish a commercial beachhead on the Delaware, sail back to Sweden, and then return with reinforcements to consolidate the Swedish position in the territory the Indians had deeded to him. The legality of the ownership of the land would have to be resolved on diplomatic levels between the Swedish ambassador to the United Netherlands and the States General, and Oxenstierna and his associates would have to handle that issue.

Shortly after Minuit's arrival he ordered the *Grip* to sail to Virginia to trade her cargo for tobacco. Presumably Andrian Jöransen was still in command of the *Grip*, and when the vessel docked at Jamestown the English Governor William Berkeley said he did not have authority to trade "duty free" with the Swedes for tobacco. He recommended that the Swedes request permission from the King of England to trade with Virginia. This was not meant as a slight to the Swedes because even at that early date England wanted to exercise control over shipments of Virginia tobacco. The *Grip* remained for about ten days, filled her casks with fresh water, and sailed back to the Minquas Kill without tobacco. The crew was doubtless surprised to see the progress made in the construction of Fort Christina. An English report of the voyage of the *Grip* to Virginia has been misinterpreted by many historians to mean that both the *Grip* and *Kalmar Nyckel* made a landing in Jamestown prior to arriving in the Delaware, but this is negated by the dates of the voyage.

About May 20, the *Grip* lifted anchor again, but this time her destination was the West Indies waters, where Minuit hoped to increase the yield of the American venture by seizing a Spanish bark carrying gold or silver. That kind of prize could pay for the entire expedition. He elected to remain with the *Kalmar Nyckel* to complete the construction at Fort Christina with the members of the crew and the soldiers; he also wanted to barter further with the Indians so that he could return to Sweden with as many furs as possible.

The *Grip* had not yet returned in June, but the fort was completed and Minuit felt the time had come to sail back home. He had been gone fron Gothenburg more than seven months, and he knew that the New Sweden Company's officials were anxious about the vessels. He still had hogsheads of liquors and casks of wines in his cargo to dispose of before leaving American waters, and he charted his return voyage via the Caribbean, where he expected to unload and take on a cargo of tobacco. Minuit left twenty-four men at Fort Christina, including Måns Kling, who was placed in command, with Hendrick Huygen in charge of the storehouse. No enrollment list has been found giving all the names and occupations of the others who are referred to in general terms as "soldiers," which should not be taken literally. All were doubtless familiar with the use of swords and firearms, but some were workmen and others were farmers assigned to cultivate edibles. It seems logical that one of the barber-surgeons remained to care for their health. It is reasonable to surmise that all of them were capable of handling muskets in the event of an Indian attack. That step seemed unlikely because Minuit had gone to great pains to establish amicable relations with the Lenape chiefs, and he had laid a basis for trade that was just as advantageous to the Indians as it was to the Swedes.

Minuit brought seed grain from Sweden that the men planted near the fort after the land was cleared and hoed up by hand since there were no horses or oxen in the first expedition. Thus, in addition to trading with the Indians, keeping peace with the Dutch garrison at Fort Nassau, and maintaining the American base in Swedish hands, Kling and his men were expected to plant crops. Minuit undoubtedly warned Kling that winters could be severe in the Delaware valley, so Kling, in turn, instructed Huygen to store and preserve victuals for future use without tolerating waste.

After Minuit's departure the *Grip* again returned to Fort Christina, but not in time to sail home in company with the *Kalmar Nyckel*. Very little is known of her adventures in the waters of the West Indies except that she did not take any Spanish prizes and did not obtain any gold or silver. She brought with her from one of the islands a Negro originally from Angola in Africa named Anthony, who was left at Fort Christina with the other men—the first recorded black in New Sweden. Whether he was a free man or had been purchased as a slave is not known, but his name is listed in the roster of the colony nine years later without his name linked to that of an owner.

Due to contrary winds the *Grip* was unable to leave Fort Christina until late April of 1639. She took aboard a quantity of furs that Huygen had purchased from the Indians after the *Kalmar Nyckel*'s departure, and she also had tobacco in her cargo obtained in the West Indies.

After Minuit left Fort Christina on the *Kalmar Nyckel*, he sailed to Saint Christopher, one of the small Leeward Islands in the West Indies. There he exchanged the liquor and wines he had on board for a cargo of tobacco. After loading the tobacco aboard ship, he and Captain van der Water were invited by the captain of a ship from Rotterdam to visit his vessel, the *Flying Deer*, then lying at anchor in the harbor along with numerous other craft of various sizes. The records do not tell us whether or not Minuit was acquainted with the skipper of the Dutch vessel, but possibly he or van der Water had met the skipper before. In any event it was intended as a social visit where men of the sea raise glasses and spin yarns about their voyages, and Minuit had much to tell about the first Swedish expedition. While they were visiting together on the Dutch vessel, a hurricane arose and swept through the harbor. Twenty of the ships at anchor were driven out to sea. Many of them perished; some lost one or more of their masts; others, like the *Kalmar Nyckel*, also caught in the storm, returned undamaged.

The *Flying Deer* never returned. Her crew and captain, and the captain's two guests, were never seen again. So ended the life of Peter Minuit, who achieved his ambition to found a New Sweden but never returned to Stockholm to make a long-awaited report to his superiors and plan a larger expedition with women and children.

Minuit's instructions stated that "if it should happen that the good Lord come to fetch you," Michel Symonssen, first mate on the *Kalmar Nyckel*, should succeed him. Symonssen waited in the harbor for a number of days for information about the *Flying Deer*. Finally convinced that she had sunk, he took command and brought the vessel back to Gothenburg. When Minuit arrived in Saint Christopher he had in his possession a map he had made, sketches of Fort Christina and the two houses built there, as well as other papers and probably a journal of the voyage. Those precious documents were evidently sent to Admiral Fleming, but they are now missing. No biography of Minuit has ever been written and no portrait of him is known to exist.

When the investors in the New Sweden Company balanced the accounts of the first expedition they found that the two vessels had brought back a total of 1,769 beaver pelts, 314 otter pelts, 132 bear pelts, and miscellaneous skins that were sold in Holland for a total of 15,426 florins. The tobacco on the two vessels was sold in Sweden for 18,649 florins, surprisingly bringing in more cash than the skins. Total income from the voyage was 34,075 florins, but the cost of the expedition, including cargoes, wages, and supplies, was in excess of 46,000 florins. The Swedish investors believed that the company was off to a very promising beginning, even though expenses exceeded sales, but the Dutch investors, including Blommaert, were disappointed because their expectations were much higher. They knew the West India Company had been importing furs from the New Netherland amounting to 50,000 and 60,000 florins annually, as well as large quantities of tobacco. It is impossible to relate those amounts to modern American money, but the annual importation of furs alone to Holland may have represented the buying power of half a million modern inflated American dollars, or more.

The voyages of the *Kalmar Nyckel* and the *Grip* dramatically brought to the attention of investors in the New Sweden Company the tremendous opportunities in the tobacco market. Tobacco was slow to make its way into the Swedish market, and prior to 1630 its use was very limited, having first been brought into the country by Dutch sailors or soldiers. In 1633 a dissertation was published in Sweden on the medicinal properties of the tobacco plant, a belief that had already run its course in Spain, France, and England.

The first tobacco brought to those countries from America was considered a kind of Indian wonder drug. The leaves steeped in hot water were used as a poultice for headaches and a cure for bruises and toothaches. Tobacco leaves were rolled up to make crude cigars and also shredded and smoked in pipes to purge the stomach, clear the lungs of congestions, and bring relief from coughs and colds. The tobacco leaves were also finely powdered and snuffed up the nostrils for health purposes; some persons believed that it provoked sneezing which cleared out the brains! In the court of France snuffing became an elegant social practice having nothing to do with ailments, and from there the custom spread to Italy, England, and other countries where French customs were imitated.

As tobacco became more popular, it was smoked, snuffed, and chewed for recreation and pleasure; the alleged medicinal properties became incidental. Sweden was going through that transition in belief about the value of tobacco when the New Sweden Company was being organized. Minuit knew that tobacco was a sleeping economic giant ready to awaken and enslave Swedish consumers. What had happened in Holland would be repeated in Sweden. As the Swedes were being habituated as inveterate consumers of the tobacco plant, Minuit made certain the New Sweden Company possessed the exclusive rights to its importation. Having personally raised tobacco in New Amsterdam, Minuit was aware that it was a difficult plant to grow. Neither the Swedish soil nor weather were conducive to raising it. Tobacco would soon be Sweden's principal import from America.

Swedish merchants were also eager to import all the furs they could get their hands on, although the major market was not in Sweden itself. The big demand was in Holland, Poland, and Germany, where willing buyers awaited all the furs the Swedes could offer for sale. The first expedition proved the point that Minuit had made in his original letter to Oxenstierna offering his services—Sweden's most lucrative commercial opportunity was not then in copper but in the importation of furs and tobacco from the New World. Minuit's life was tragically snuffed out before his big dream was fully realized, for he also visualized a transplantation of Swedish society to New Sweden. That was why he was so intent upon buying land from the Indians.

3. RIDDER TAKES CHARGE OF THE COLONY

Peter Minuit's untimely death left Chancellor Oxenstierna, Samuel Blommaert, Baron Spiring, and Admiral Fleming to carry on with the plans for the expansion of New Sweden. They had all expected Minuit to command the second expedition. His death was a tragic loss to the New Sweden Company. Admiral Fleming, who held the position of president or director of the company, initiated discussions with his associates about a second voyage before the *Kalmar Nyckel* returned with the news of Minuit's death. When he learned of the tragedy, Fleming knew that Minuit would be a hard man to replace, but the information in Minuit's journal, the Indian deeds, and Minuit's drawings that Michel Symonssen brought back on the *Kalmar Nyckel* encouraged him to continue with his plans. It was as though Minuit reached back from his watery grave to reassure him that there was a place in America for the Swedes even though they were latecomers.

Fleming's inclination was to send a larger expedition than the first one, but Blommaert and the other Dutch investors refused to put up more money. While his proposition was under discussion, the *Grip* returned to Gothenburg, and the sums still due the officers and sailors were a further drain on the company's treasury. Nevertheless, the Swedish investors favored a second voyage without delay, but they wanted matching funds from their Dutch partners.

After the *Grip*'s return, a storm in August of 1639 tore her loose from the two anchors supposed to hold her fast in the harbor. She was driven on a sandbar by the winds and wrecked. Her cannon were salvaged, but she would not float and must have foundered since there is no further reference to her. The *Grip* was not an irreparable loss, but it was nevertheless costly.

After considerable discussion, a decision was made to send the *Kalmar Nyckel* alone on the second expedition, and a Dutch skipper, Captain Cornelis van Vliet, was placed in command of the vessel. Lieutenant Peter Hollander Ridder, of Dutch or low German descent, who had served the Swedish admiralty in Sweden and Finland, was selected to replace Måns Kling as the commander of Fort Christina. Another Dutchman, Joost van Langdonk, was employed as the commissary to replace Hendrick Huygen in New Sweden, and Gregorius van Dyck, whose name would later become important in the colony, went as the assistant commissary. The first mate and most of the sailors were Dutchmen hired by Fleming in Holland, but there was a Lutheran minister on the expedition and he was a Swede—the Reverend Reorus Torkillus.

Efforts were made to reinforce the colony with artisans such as blacksmiths, shoemakers, carpenters, bricklayers, and the like, especially those who had wives who could cook, wash, and brew beer for the men. Such craftsmen were enjoying a comfortable living in Sweden and did not want to leave their homeland. In order to enlist colonists a proposal was made and accepted by the Crown that deserters from the army and soldiers who had committed slight misdemeanors should be drafted for service in America, accompanied by their families. Soldiers were permitted to return to Sweden in two years if they so desired. Each was to be supplied initially with two daler in copper money, lower in value than the silver daler. One-and-one-half daler constituted a riksdaler, which was equal to two-and-one-half florins.

There is no listing of how many soldiers, freemen, or hired hands boarded the *Kalmar Nyckel* on the second voyage, but it is certain that there were women and children in the expedition. The names of some of the passengers who became prominent in the colony are known, names such as Peter Gunnarrson Rambo, Anders Larsson Dalbo, Anders Svensson Bonde, Måns Andersson, and Sven Gunnarsson. Four mares, two young horses, farm implements, food, clothing, and merchandise for the Indian trade were also taken aboard.

The *Kalmar Nyckel* set sail in the beginning of September 1639, and the vessel had bad luck from the beginning. She developed severe leaks while in the North Sea and had to seek haven in the port of Mendemblik in North Holland for repairs. Most of the cargo had to be unloaded so that master carpenters could work to make the vessel seaworthy. After a long delay the cargo was taken aboard and the vessel went to sea again, and again developed leaks that forced her to limp back to Mendemblik for the second time. The trouble was due to old bolts and nails that had rusted and corroded from exposure to salt water, allowing the wood joints to separate.

After leaving Mendemblik for the second time the leaks recurred, and the ship had to be taken to Amsterdam for further repairs. Admiral Spiring came in person to inspect her and found that faulty workmanship at Mendemblik was the cause of the trouble and that obviously Captain van Vliet had been negligent in supervising the carpenters. The captain was also accused by members of the crew of fraud and disobeying orders. Spiring examined the cargo and found that the captain was, in fact, guilty of cheating the company. Spiring discharged him and hired a new captain in Amsterdam, another Dutchman, named Poewel Jansen. On February 7, 1640, the *Kalmar Nyckel* at long last was ready to leave Holland for America. The total cost of the expedition had now reached 15,840 daler, equal to 24,000 guilders.

The remainder of the voyage was also an unhappy one. Ridder and van Langdonk had differences of opinion; Captain Jansen, van Langdonk, and some of the crew members drank to excess; discipline aboard ship was lacking; and the Reverend Torkillus was harassed by the Dutch skipper and sailors, all Calvinists having a holy hate for Lutherans. Storms were encountered in the Atlantic, and many of the passengers became seasick.

Meanwhile at Fort Christina the twenty-four men left there by Minuit had long been scanning the horizon for signs of a ship sailing into the Minquas Kill with Swedish colors flying from her mast. What a welcome sight the *Kalmar Nyckel* must have been when she glided in on April 17, 1640, after having left Gothenburg almost eight months before. It was *their* vessel, and they recognized her silhouette before she reached the fort. They were elated when she landed with reinforcements, merchandise and food, a few domestic animals, women and children, and a minister of the gospel, the first Lutheran pastor in New Sweden, to conduct religious services and serve them communion. Needless to say the passengers and crew were also exuberant to reach their destination and to greet fellow Dutchmen and fellow Swedes when they went ashore at "the Rocks."

Måns Kling served the company well as commander of Fort Christina in a difficult assignment, where contention naturally developed between Swedes and Dutch living together in close quarters. He had made good use of the sloop that Minuit left with him to barter with the Lenape at their villages along the Schuylkill. Minquas trading parties also brought beaver pelts from the Susquehanna country to Fort Christina, and Kling managed to keep on friendly terms with both tribes although they were not friendly toward each other. Minquas war parties had attacked the Lenape and burned some of their towns before the Swedes had arrived in America. The large inventory of trade merchandise Minuit left for his use was a major factor in cementing amicable relations with both tribes, because the Swedes were able to offer the Indians more goods for their pelts than could the Dutch. At New Amsterdam, where the Dutch accumulated furs for shipment to Holland, Governor Kieft wrote to his superiors that the fur trade on the South River at Fort Nassau was "entirely ruined by the Swedes." That was an exaggeration, but there is no question that the Swedish competition was injurious to the fur business of the West India Company. Kieft's forces were not strong enough to permit a punitive attack on

Fort Christina, nor would the officials of the West India Company have approved of aggression at a time when friendly relations existed between the two governments. Moreover, at that time in history Sweden was a more powerful military nation than Holland. Kieft tried persuasion, hoping to convince Kling and his men to vacate, but Kling had his orders to hold the fort. He refused to leave.

When the *Kalmar Nyckel* was ready to lift anchor for her return to Sweden on or about May 14, 1640, the records say that she left with a "large cargo." Doubtless the main product she carried were bundles of furs, especially beaver pelts, that Kling had obtained from the Indians. The likelihood is that the vessel also carried tobacco purchased from private English or Dutch merchants who came to Fort Christina in their barks and sloops looking for business. The men stationed at Fort Christina had not planted any tobacco, because their main concern was in raising edible grains and vegetables for their own consumption. They supplemented their food supply by killing wild game, catching fish, and trading with the Lenape for corn. Since they all survived two years at Fort Christina, the food supply must have been adequate, although living conditions were rigorous, especially in the cold weather when they were confined to the two small log buildings in the fort. Deprived of the companionship of wives or sweethearts and the sound of children's voices, the winters must have been lonely.

Hendrick Huygen, Måns Kling, and some of the others went back home on the *Kalmar Nyckel*, but how many of the twenty-four left and how many remained at the fort is not known. Anthony, the black Angoler, stayed in the colony, and it seems likely that Klas (also spelled Clas) Jansson was among those who remained. Since there are no figures on the number of settlers that Ridder brought to New Sweden, the size of the population at the beginning of Ridder's administration is unknown. The total number of men, women, and children, though, was very small—perhaps forty or fifty, at most.

The population figures and other details were recorded at the time, but the old papers disintegrated, were destroyed by ro-

dents and fires, or were lost or discarded. It is known that
Måns Kling took with him on his return to Sweden a report and
several letters written by Ridder as well as a journal and letters
written by Gregorius van Dyck. After the *Kalmar Nyckel* arrived in Sweden, Hendrick Huygen made a special trip to
Stockholm to make a verbal report to Admiral Fleming that
fully informed the company management of the status of the
colony. Undoubtedly the substance of his report was that good
progress had been made, that the future looked promising, and
that he was so optimistic he intended to return to New Sweden
with his family on the next expedition. Having been in the
colony for two years he spoke with authority; the Swedish
investors were pleased with what they heard. Their Dutch partners were less enthusiastic. Some were beginning to feel that
they were being unpatriotic by subsidizing the Swedish company. It was no secret that the stockholders in the Dutch West
India Company in Amsterdam were unhappy when they read
Governor Kieft's reports about Swedish competition in the fur
business.

After the *Kalmar Nyckel*'s cargo was brought ashore—and
accomodations found for the passengers—Ridder turned over
the keys of the storehouse in the fort to van Langdonk. The
responsibility of the commissary, or commis, as the title was
abbreviated, not only included supervision and dispensation of
food and supplies owned by the company, but also the procure-
ment of corn from the Indians and needed supplies from Dutch
and English merchants. The commissary also kept a perpetual inventory and maintained account books. Van Langdonk
and Ridder were impressed that the vastland north and northeast
of the fort was well suited for agriculture and cattle raising. Of
course, the settlers still had no cattle—only the mares and
horses brought by the *Kalmar Nyckel*—and since the seed grain
had rotted during the long voyage, there was no urgency in
plowing up the earth until new seeds were available.

Ridder attempted to use his manpower to mend breaks in the
walls and ramparts of the fort. Within the palisaded area he

erected three more log houses to accomodate the settlers, and he
moved the two cabins Minuit had built to the east side of the
fort. He also erected a new storehouse and a stable for the
horses. He complained in a letter he wrote to Chancellor
Oxenstierna that he lacked skilled workmen, and he recommended that experienced carpenters be sent on the next expedition, as well as a pair of oxen, cows, "glass windows," hemp,
salt, brandy, and seeds to raise rye, barley, beans, peas, cabbages, turnips, and parsnips.

As a military man, Ridder was not impressed with the location
of Fort Christina, which he believed was too far up the Minquas
Kill to command the Delaware River; ships going up and down
the river were beyond the range of the fort's cannon. Minuit
was well aware of that when he selected the site, but his
objective was not to control ship traffic in the river, but to avoid
a clash with the Dutch while at the same time blocking off one
of the arteries leading to the Minquas country. If he had dared
to start building Fort Christina on the Delaware River, Kieft
might not have exercised restraint, even at the risk of provoking
an affront with Sweden.

Ridder had no authority to erect another fort, even if he had
qualified workmen to do so, but he did the next best thing,
which was to extend the bounds of New Sweden. He gave the
Lenape trade goods for which they signed a deed conveying
land from the Schuylkill up to the Sankikans and from Duck
Creek south to Cape Henlopen. That extension of the lands
Minuit "bought" from the Indians meant that New Sweden now
included all the western side of the Delaware River from present-
day Lewes as far north as Trenton, encompassing all of present-
day Philadelphia and suburbs. By deeding that land to Ridder
the Lenape were unknowingly dispossessing themselves of the
sites of some of their largest communities. Of course, that was
not their intention, for, as previously discussed, they merely
thought they were showing hospitality by granting "use" rights
to the Swedes.

Up to this time the Swedes had not negotiated with the
Lenape for lands in New Jersey, and as of 1641 there was no

European occupation on the east side of the Delaware River except the Dutch garrison at Fort Nassau. It has already been pointed out that this fort, erected in 1626, predated the building of Fort Christina. Ridder went upstream several times in the sloop to inspect the country, and on two occasions the Dutch at Fort Nassau fired at the little vessel, but the shots seem to have been warnings because they did no damage. The commandant at the fort also sent a protest to Ridder, repeating what Kieft had told Minuit—the whole river belonged to the Dutch West India Company. Fort Nassau was only weakly garrisoned, and Ridder could have withstood a Dutch attack on Fort Christina but none materialized. Ridder's instructions were to keep on as good terms as possible with the Dutch, which is what he tried to do. Then something happened that tended temporarily to draw the Swedes and Dutch closer to each other, a common foe appeared in the Delaware—the English.

A settlement was formed in Connecticut called the New Haven Colony, actually an offshoot of the Massachusetts Bay Colony, although its success was due to Puritan newcomers from England. The fur trade was one of its principal aims. Expansion was slow, and the fur trade did not develop as the founders anticipated because the coastal beaver population had been depleted by traders from Plymouth and the aggressive Dutch from New Amsterdam. Furs were important for the merchants of the New Haven Colony to build up credit in London, using the pelts to accumulate bills of exchange to invest in American commodities. New Haven began trading not only with Boston and London, but also with New Amsterdam, Virginia, and the Barbadoes. Finally the merchants decided to seek beaver pelts in the Delaware valley. The Delaware Company of New Haven was formed with the financial backing of New Haven's governor, Theophilus Eaton, and a number of other investors, including two active and influential promoters, George Lamberton and Nathaniel Turner.

In the spring of 1641 when Ridder was expanding the land area of New Sweden, Lamberton and Turner, with twelve other Englishmen, sailed up the Delaware in a sloop well provided with European trade merchandise. They had been authorized by the Delaware Company to barter for beaver pelts and to purchase land from the Indian owners for establishing a colony. The Englishmen explored the Delaware and its navigable tributaries, and they made contact with the Indians to barter for furs, which was detrimental to both Swedes and Dutch.

The Englishmen also purchased land from the Indians as a site for their colony at a place the Lenape called Watcessit on the stream known to the Dutch as the Varkens Kill ("Hog's Creek"), present-day Salem River. The stream was then navigable to shallops for several miles, and larger vessels could near present-day Salem. Even though Lamberton and Turner left half miles from the stream's confluence with the Delaware. The precise location of the English settlement at Watcessit has never been found, but it was along the banks of the Salem River at or near present-day Salem. Even though Lamberton and Turner left only a handful of Englishmen at Watcessit when they returned to New Haven, Ridder and Kieft both strongly resented the English intrusion. Ridder sailed across the river to the Varkens Kill and registered his protest, which Lamberton and Turner ignored. Ridder had no authority to use force to oust the English, and since Sweden and England were at peace aggressive action on his part was ill-advised. During that confrontation with the English, Ridder conferred with some of the Lenape chiefs living on the east side of the Delaware, and he negotiated a purchase of land from what was then called Narraticons Creek, present-day Raccoon Creek, as far south as Cape May, extending New Sweden to part of New Jersey. But the tidewater land he purchased was the identical land that Lamberton and Turner claimed they had bought. Ridder's refutation was that he bought the land from the chiefs three days *before* the English bought it.

Once again it is very clear that the differences in the concept of land tenure led to confusion and misunderstanding. It was certainly not the intention of the Lenape to defraud Dutch and Swedes by selling them the same property, nor did they intend the transactions to divest themselves of rights to the land—they were generously sharing its use with the newcomers. The documents covering those negotiations with the Indians have been lost, and no copies were made of what was agreed on. Even the bounds of the land are vague. The northern and southern bounds were given according to verbal reports of the transactions, and the Delaware River was obviously the western boundary, but the eastern bound is not known.

Despite Ridder's claim of prior purchase, Lamberton and Turner returned the next year (1642) to reinforce the settlement at Watcessit and to acquire land from the Lenape for additional settlements. The Delaware Company of New Haven now realized that furs were not the only profitable product that the Delaware valley yielded; the English settlers found that they could raise tobacco in southern New Jersey's soil. They also learned that one of the best trading places for furs was along the Schuylkill River, which was still unsettled by either Dutch or Swedes. There they could trade with the Lenape at the Indian villages and also barter with trading parties of Minquas enroute to Fort Nassau with beaver pelts. One of the several trails leading to the Susquehanna snaked overland to a terminal on Kingsessing Creek, and if English traders were there to intercept them it was unnecessary for the Minquas to go any farther.

James Waye, a member of the Lamberton-Turner expedition from New Haven in 1642 stated that the English bought land from the Lenape on the Schuylkill River for forty pounds sterling in trade goods. There they built a blockhouse and dwellings as a base for trade with the Indians, offering better bargains than the natives could get from either Dutch or Swedes. Now Ridder was the victim who experienced a sharp decline in the fur business, but he and Kieft laid aside their differences in meeting the English threat. Kieft dispatched orders to the commandant at Fort Nassau on May 22, 1642, to proceed against the English trespassers. To reinforce the garrison at Fort Nassau he also sent two armed sloops from New Amsterdam. The Dutch commandant was ordered to instruct the English to leave but not to shed any blood. If they refused to depart he was instructed to take them forcibly aboard the vessels, without injury to them or their personal effects, and bring them to New Amsterdam. After the English vacated their houses and the trading post he was ordered to "lay waste that place."

Kieft's orders were fully obeyed. James Waye wrote that "the Dutch came in and burnt our houses or Garrison & carried us away prisoners to New Haven in New England. . . ." That was the end of the English settlement on the Schuylkill. It might be noted that the first European settlement within the bounds of the present state of Pennsylvania was made by Englishmen, not Swedes or Dutch. The irony is that the Dutch were the aggressors in removing the English, not the Swedes, but the English settlement was on land Ridder had bought from the Indians as an extension of New Sweden. Of course, the Dutch didn't accept Ridder's purchase as bona fide; they considered the Schuylkill territory as part of New Netherland.

The approximately dozen English farm families at Watcessit on the Varkens Kill were not molested by the Dutch attackers. Since they were not a factor in the fur trade, Kieft evidently saw no reason to disturb them. Ridder probably felt there were too few to do any harm, and if they chanced to raise tobacco in quantity it would give him another source of supply. In the meantime, he was doing his utmost to encourage the settlers at Fort Christina to cultivate tobacco to meet the increasing demand in Sweden.

In Stockholm during the first year of Ridder's administration the New Sweden Company was planning a new expedition to send additional settlers and supplies to him. Two vessels were prepared for the voyage, the *Kalmar Nyckel*, making her third voyage to New Sweden, and a companion ship, the *Charitas* (*Charity*), known to the Swedes as a flot. The latter was a large freight vessel that commonly was armed with only two guns so that the weight and space required by armaments and ammunition could be used for cargo and livestock. Måns Kling and Hendrick Huygen reported the critical need for farm animals in the colony, and it was decided to send horses, goats, sheep, cattle, and a large quantity of farming implements. Huygen was

LEGEND OF A LENAPE VILLAGE:

THE INDIAN VILLAGE WAS OFTEN AT THE CONFLUENCE OF TWO STREAMS FOR NATURAL PROTECTION. HUNTERS AND FISHERMEN OBTAIN FOOD — WOMEN CULTIVATE CORN FIELDS, CARRY FIREWOOD, CRUSH CORN, DRY FISH, PREPARE MEALS. THE LARGER WIGWAM HOUSED MORE THAN ONE FAMILY.

sent to Holland on behalf of the New Sweden Company to purchase the kind of supplies that he knew were needed. He consented to return to the colony as the commissary replacing van Langdonk, an incompetent man lacking the qualifications the job required and never in sympathy with the Swedes.

Kling, who had been promoted to a lieutenant, also decided to return to New Sweden for the second time, accompanied by his wife, a servant girl, and a small child. His military pay was increased to forty florins a month, which was equal to about a hundred silver daler, a very comfortable income compared to the earnings of the common soldiers cited later. The New Sweden Company was not niggardly in supporting the expedition—even though the balance sheet of the company showed a large deficit, more than 36,000 florins were spent before the two ships raised their anchors.

Although the New Sweden Company sponsored the expedition of the *Kalmar Nyckel* and the *Charitas*, the government of Sweden took an active and lively interest in the preparation because it was hoped that "New Sweden would in time redound to the service and honor of the Swedish Crown and to the prosperity and improvement of its citizens." There is little doubt that Chancellor Oxenstierna and his associates were now thinking of New Sweden in terms of a transplantation of Swedish life and culture to the New World rather than just a trading venture. That meant political expansion of the empire and also the opportunity of spreading Lutheranism to the heathen Indians. The records do not reveal how the Dutch investors in the New Sweden Company reacted to what they would have considered Swedish imperialism, but it goes without saying that it was inimical to the best interests of the United Netherlands.

The Swedish government did its best to encourage Swedes to migrate to America to strengthen the colony, but colonists were as much a problem for the third expedition as they were for the second. Not enough interest could be generated to induce Swedish families to pull up stakes and leave their homeland. Then a new idea took shape. Why not punish those forest-burning Finns for disobeying Swedish laws by sending them to America?

Moreover, were they not also infracting laws against hunting by shooting elks for their hides and then allowing the animals' bodies to lie and rot in the woods? Strong prejudices existed against the Finns then living in Sweden, because it was known that many of them slipped out of Finland during the Thirty Years' War to escape conscription in the Swedish army and then lost themselves in the dense forests of northern and central Sweden. In the autumn of 1636 an order was issued commanding all "Finnish vagrants" to leave Sweden and go back home. "Honest and industrious Finns" who could prove they were settled down and living like Swedish farmers were supposed to be immune from the law, but the governor of Örebro, an inland town west of Stockholm, wrote the government that there were vagrant Finns in his district who could not be trusted to settle down. He received a prompt reply telling him to persuade the Finns to migrate to New Sweden, where people were needed, with their wives and children. He was told to assure them that there was an abundance of forests they could burn in America and plenty of wild animals to shoot.

While the effort was being made to round up itinerant Finns, an incident occurred involving four Finns sentenced to have their property confiscated and to serve in the Swedish army for burning the forests. The four agreed that if they were released from service in the army they would go to New Sweden, and permission was given for their transfer. Their property was supposed to be restored if they appeared at Gothenburg ready for the voyage.

The authorities also sent Måns Kling to recruit colonists, especially any roving Finns, in the ancient province of Dalarne northwest of Stockholm. Having had personal experience in America he was encouraged to describe New Sweden as a beautiful and productive country. If they would not go willingly, he was authorized to capture the forest-destroyers and hold them in readiness at Stockholm for the departure of the *Charitas*. The plans called for the *Charitas* to sail from Stockholm and join the *Kalmar Nyckel* at Gothenburg, where other colonists were getting ready for the voyage.

When the *Charitas* left Stockholm there were thirty-five persons aboard, including Lieutenant Kling and his family. Some were Finns and others Swedes, although their ethnic identities were not stated. Apparently individual arrangements were made with each prospective colonist; some were to be paid by the company as employees; some went on their own; some were given a small cash bounty before boarding the vessel. It was a rare instance where the names were recorded and general comments made about the persons themselves. Those comments have been abbreviated below to give the reader some understanding of the character of the colonists on that expedition:

Eight of the men, servants, laborers, or soldiers, were each given a suit of clothes and a salary of twenty Riksdaler per year. Their names were Ivert Hindricksson, Olof Påvelsson, Per Johannson, Johan Ericksson, Anders Hansson, Jacob Sprint, Paul Jöransson, and Axel Stille.

Three boys, each to have a yearly salary of ten Riksdaler— Henrick Matsson, Olof Erickson, and Johan, no last name given.* A fourth boy, Påfvel Schal, son of a Stockholm baker, goes without receiving any pay. [Possibly it was intended to have those boys serve as apprentices.]

Mans Svensson Lom, a tailor, who had been a lieutenant, accompanied by his wife, two teenage daughters, and a small son. He receives no salary, apparently intending to earn his own living.

Olof Stille, a mill-maker, or millwright, with a wife and two small children. He receives no salary, but will be paid for what he does. [At that time there was no gristmill in New Sweden; possibly it was intended that he build one.]

Mats Hansson, one of Klas Fleming's servants, who had committed an unnamed offense, was sent as punishment. He will receive food and clothing from the company but no pay.

Per Kock [Peter Cock] an imprisoned soldier, sent to

----

*Peter S. Craig identifies him as Johan Andersson who later adopted the name Stalcop.

serve out his term, who is to receive food and clothing but no pay.

Karl Johansson, a bookkeeper, deported as punishment for an unstated misdeed. He is also supposed to serve at times as a soldier. [It is known that he was a Finn.]

Eskel Larsson, a deserter from the army, sent for punishment.

Herr Christoffer, a Lutheran preacher, who will receive board but no pay. He goes for experience and to try his luck. [While in New Sweden he assisted the Reverend Torkillus, but he returned to Sweden again in 1643 and then received pay for his service.]

Gustaf Strahl, a young nobleman, who also wants to try his luck and get experience. He will receive board but nothing more.

Mickel Jonsson (Bolm), an adventurer, who wants to try his luck and seeks no pay.

Mats Hansson and his wife [a different person from the one shown above]. He goes to be a constable at Fort Christina at a salary not yet fixed, and also wants to start a farm or a tobacco plantation. [He was the brother of Anders Hansson named above.]

Lars Markusson, hired to work in the tobacco fields. Receives a suit and an annual salary of twenty Riksdaler.

There is no record of the names or number of passengers at Gothenburg who were waiting to join those who arrived on the *Charitas*, although Hendrick Huygen was already aboard the *Kalmar Nyckel*, where the sailors and officers were almost ready to sail. Probably the majority of the passengers on the *Charitas* transferred to the *Kalmar Nyckel*, thus allowing more space for the livestock and cargo on the freighter.

Transporting livestock by sailboat on seventeenth-century trans-Atlantic voyages was a major and costly undertaking. Individual stalls had to be built with a thick layer of sand as litter. Large quantities of hay and oats were carried to feed the animals during the long voyage, and tanks holding fresh water were stored below the main deck. Farm hands familiar with livestock took care of the frightened animals as the vessels tossed on the waves and encountered storms, as the two ships did on the three-month voyage. The highest priority was given to keeping the animals alive and well, because horses were needed in the colony to draw plows and haul loads, and cows carrying their unborn calves would later produce milk to make cheese and other dairy products needed to feed the soldiers and colonists. No wool was available in New Sweden, and the timid sheep were pampered in every possible way to enable them to withstand an ocean voyage in storms that often frightened the strongest of men.

On that voyage the *Kalmar Nyckel* served principally as a carrier of personnel and a warship to protect the *Charitas* from freebooters. Neither vessel carried gold or silver, but their animals and cargoes constituted commodities that a privateer could seize and readily sell in the Caribbean Islands. The two vessels left Gothenburg in July, the *Kalmar Nyckel* under the command of Andrian Jansen, a Dutchman from Saardam, and the *Charitas* under the command of Jan Jochimsen from Kappell, Schleswig-Holstein. The first mate on the *Charitas* was the Scotchman Jacob Evertssen Sandelin, who had been the second mate on the *Kalmar Nyckel*'s maiden voyage to New Sweden. The majority of the sailors and soldiers on that voyage appear to have been Swedes, although there were also a few Dutch.

The colonists at Fort Christina were overjoyed on November 7, 1641, to see the two Swedish vessels entering the mouth of the Minquas Kill, and Ridder was delighted when the cargoes were unloaded with foodstuffs, bags of seeds, tools, building supplies, merchandise for the Indian trade, and the long-awaited farm animals. Almost everything he had requested was on the vessels, and, generally speaking, the new colonists provided most of the skills then needed. Having endured one cold winter at the fort, Ridder was anxious to house the new families properly before the snow fell, and the small buildings within the fort were already overcrowded. New log cabins were built outside the fort on plots selected for settlement, and new land was cleared and prepared for spring planting. Some of the animals died during the voyage, but five horses, eight cows, five sheep, and two goats were landed alive, and shelter had to be provided for them. There were already a number of pigs in the colony, which had been taken over previously or been bought in New Amsterdam. The pigs bred rapidly. Many of them ran wild, foraging in the woods. Often they were shot, and the pork smoked and salted for winter use.

By the time the *Kalmar Nyckel* and *Charitas* were ready to return to Sweden on November 29, 1641, the colonists had made good progress building their cabins, and Lieutenant Kling had reorganized and strengthened the garrison at the fort with the soldiers who came with him. Gregorius van Dyck and Joost van Langdonk returned to Sweden on one of the ships. Ridder was not sorry to see the latter go because he was a troublemaker, an inefficient commis, and, as a Calvinist, an abuser of the Reverend Torkillus and the other Swedish Lutherans. On the other hand, van Dyck was a competent executive who returned to the colony less than two years later. The movement of individuals back and forth between Sweden and America kept the company better informed than is generally realized.

The *Kalmar Nyckel* and the *Charitas* left Fort Christina with almost empty holds. There were only six beaver pelts in the storehouse when the two ships arrived because the New Haven English had ruined the Indian trade that year, and, of course, there was no tobacco crop to export. On the return voyage the *Charitas* obtained 1,278 barrels of salt in France, which was largely sold in Finland, where there was a good market for salt. Salt was an important import in both Sweden and Finland, usually coming from Spain and Portugal. Its main use was as a preservative.

Very little is known about the religious life in the colony during the Ridder administration, although it is certain that religion was taken very seriously because the worship of God was given the highest priority among both rich and poor in both Sweden and Holland. There can be no question that the Reverend Torkillus conducted Lutheran services in the fort with pro-

CROP FARMING

WOOD TOOTH HARROW

MAIZE AND
TOBACCO

HARVESTING

WORKING THE GROUND

HAYING

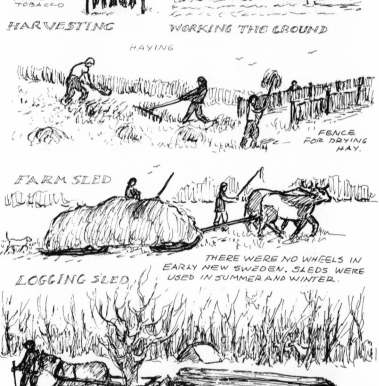

FENCE
FOR DRYING
HAY.

FARM SLED

THERE WERE NO WHEELS IN
EARLY NEW SWEDEN. SLEDS WERE
USED IN SUMMER AND WINTER.

LOGGING SLED

scribed regularity. Although Herr Christopher (Christoffer) was not specifically sent to assist Torkillus, he also helped to look after the religious needs of the colonists. It seems likely that in the latter part of Ridder's administration some kind of chapel was erected, either inside or outside the fort, to accomodate the Lutheran congregation, but no description or drawing of it has been preserved.

In the spring and summer of 1642, grain was sprouting from the fresh furrows in the fields around the fort; vegetables of various kinds were growing; and tobacco patches could be seen here and there. New Sweden also had its first mill that year—a windmill that supplied power to the millstones that ground the grain into flour. Windmills to most Americans have a Dutch connotation, and it is true that windmills were found throughout Holland, but they were also built in Sweden. The Swedish windmill at Fort Christina was the first in the Middle Atlantic states, although the Puritans had earlier built windmills in Massachusetts. Could it be that Olof Stille, the millwright, and the first member of that family in America, had something to do with building the mill, or was it erected by one of the unnamed Finns forcibly exiled from his homeland?

4. THE PRINTZ EXPEDITION

The major Dutch financial backers of the New Sweden Company were also stockholders in the Dutch West India Company, or their associates, and their investments in a competitive company led to sharp criticism in Holland. They evidently did not feel uncomfortable when they invested in the Swedish firm because they did not suspect that Swedish rivalry in both the tobacco and fur trades would have an adverse effect on the West India Company. Governor Kieft's letters to the company's directors in Amsterdam left no doubt that Dutch business in the New Netherland was suffering from Swedish competition. It was beginning to appear that the Dutch investors in the Swedish company were being commercial traitors to their own country.

Under pressure from their countrymen, added to their own dissatisfaction with their return on investment, the Dutch stockholders decided to withdraw from the New Sweden Company. The Swedes did not object because their Dutch colleagues were continually pressing for more profits and obviously had no interest in diffusing Swedish customs and traditions to the New World. In fact, their own West India Company was so beset with commercial gain that colonization as an extension of Dutch life to the Delaware valley had never been the company's objective.

The matter was discussed in Stockholm, and it was decided that the treasury department would pay off the Dutch investors "since they are a hindrance to us." In February of 1641 an arrangement was made to return to the Dutch shareholders the capital they had originally invested, including a small interest charge. The Dutch were paid a total of 18,495 florins (7,398 Riksdaler) by the Swedish government to relinquish their claims. One of the ships owned by the South Ship Company was sold to reimburse the government, which illustrates how the company and the Swedish government were closely interrelated.

Samuel Blommaert, now no longer a shareholder, continued for a time in the employ of the New Sweden Company, which had been paying him 1,000 Riksdaler a year, plus expenses. Although he had no love for the West India Company, the mounting criticism in Amsterdam caused him to withdraw from the Swedish company the next year.

New Sweden then became exclusively a Swedish project; Fleming remained as president or director, and Chancellor Oxenstierna and Spiring retained their executive authority. Johan Beier was named the treasurer, and Hans Kramer was engaged as the "bookkeeper," a title that might more accurately be termed "chief accountant," for which he was paid an annual salary of 400 Riksdaler. That sum was probably comparable in buying power to the salary paid the head of the accounting department today in the employ of a small American firm. An Englishman, Benjamin Bonnell, who established a glass-making business in Sweden, was employed as the factor, a position somewhat similar to that of a modern sales manager. He was paid 600 daler per year plus expenses, which were considerable. He made contacts with entrepreneurs in Holland to buy tobacco and furs from the Swedish company, and he also handled the distribution of tobacco to wholesalers in Sweden. His job also called for business trips to England and elsewhere to open up new markets. Those organizational changes may not appear to be relevant to the story of New Sweden, but, to the contrary, they were of utmost importance. The success of the company depended upon the productivity of the little colony on the Delaware, and the expansion of the Swedish organization placed a greater financial responsibility on the men in charge of the company's business affairs at Fort Christina.

The financial details involved in the reorganization are somewhat complicated, but, in general terms, the resources of the
former South Ship Company, consisting largely of vessels, were
sold to make up 50 percent of the capitalization. That company,
many of whose large investors were also shareholders in the
New Sweden Company, was then practically dissolved. The
balance of the capitalization in the *new* New Sweden Company
was subscribed to by the Crown, Fleming, Spiring, and members of the rich Oxenstierna family. Chancellor Oxenstierna had
a number of close relatives, and one of his sons, Eric, then aged
eighteen and a student at Uppsala University, possessed many
of his father's qualities, later becoming a leading diplomat and
statesman. Although the New Sweden Company was technically
still a private corporation, it had, in effect, become a branch of
the government, with leading government officials making the
important decisions. Fleming, for example, retained his position
as vice-admiral in the Swedish navy and mayor of Stockholm.
Johan Beier, the treasurer, became what today would be termed
the "postmaster general" of Sweden.

The system of compensating personnel illustrates the overlap-
ping of the government and the company in a way that seems
incredibly inefficient when compared with a modern corporate
organization. As head of the postal system, Beier was paid by
the government, but he received no salary from the company as
its treasurer. Oxenstierna, Fleming, and Spiring received no
salaries as company executives. All three were on the government payroll, although discussions relative to the company and
business decisions were made on government time, sometimes
at meetings of the Council of State. Such an arrangement was
not considered irregular; it was accepted as standard operating
procedure.

Some officers and employees of the company were often
called upon to render services to the Crown without pay, and
salaries of officers and sailors assigned to the company's vessels
were usually paid by the Swedish admiralty. The military bud-
gets of soldiers and their officers who were employed in the
company's service were also paid by the government. There

seems to have been no prescribed system of cost accounting, and consistency was badly lacking. Single-entry books were kept in longhand at a time when business machinery and typewriters were still to be invented. Job descriptions were nonexistent, and laws or articles defining the conduct of the company in its relations with the government were apparently never formalized. The wonder is that the apparatus worked as well as it did for as long as it did.

Following the reorganization another expedition to New Sweden was planned under the direction of an intended empire-builder, Johan Printz. A career army officer, Printz had fought bravely in many battles and had been elevated to the rank of lieutenant-colonel. He was knighted in 1642 before leaving for New Sweden with his family, which consisted of a second wife and the children of his deceased first wife: a son, Gustaf, and five daughters, Armegot, Catharina, Christina, Elsa, and Gunilla. Much has been made in the historical literature about the size of this burly man, who is supposed to have reached the weight of 400 pounds and been, behind his back, pejoratively referred to by the Indians as Meschatz, or "large stomach." The writer was present at Fort Christina Park in Wilmington on June 27, 1938, when President Franklin D. Roosevelt accepted Carl Milles's statue on behalf of the American people. The president, who had a good sense of humor, could not resist reciting this couplet:

> No governor of Delaware
> Before or since
> Has weighed as much
> As Johan Printz.

Terms such as headstrong, overbearing, arrogant, and unjust have been used to describe Printz, and at times those adjectives were aptly applied. On the other hand, he was intelligent, resourceful, brave, shrewd, an able administrator, and a God-fearing man, son of a minister, born in a parsonage, and raised in a religious household. He did not seek the job as governor of

New Sweden, but the Council of State selected him as an executive having the necessary qualifications as leader and organizer to replace Peter Hollander Ridder. Aged fifty, Printz was the first native-born Swede to take charge of the colony, at an annual salary of 1,200 silver daler.

The Printz expedition, the fifth to New Sweden, was plagued with the perennial problem—the reluctance of Swedes to move from their country and settle in a foreign land. Since the government could not legally force law-abiding citizens to leave their homes, compulsive means were again employed to entrap those who had violated Swedish laws. Poachers, deserters from the army, insolvent debtors, forest-burning Finns, and other law-breakers were forcibly deported. Such a severe punishment seems unjust for those guilty of what today would be rated as misdemeanors, and it is well known that many respectable persons at the time were thrown into debtors' prisons and brutally punished for insignificant infractions of the law. To refer to all of the deportees to New Sweden as "criminals" is an unwarranted exaggeration.

There were some volunteers in the expedition, such as Gregorius van Dyck, returning to the colony for the second time, and two Lutheran pastors, Johan Campanius (who affixed Holm to his name because he was from Stockholm) and Israel Holg Fluviander. The latter was one of Printz's relatives, but he was not commissioned by the government as was Campanius, who received a salary while Fluviander did not. The total number of passengers fell short of expectations—probably less than a hundred men, women, and children.

There were two vessels in the expedition, the *Fama* (*Fame*), approximately equal in value to the *Kalmar Nyckel* and about the same size, and the *Swan*, a large ship described as carrying thirty-six cannon. Their cargoes consisted of tools, wine, malt for use in brewing beer, grain, pease, fish nets, muskets, shoes, clothing, horses, sheep, a few chickens, and hay to feed the livestock during the voyage. The two vessels left Gothenburg on November 11, 1642, on a long trial by wind and wave that brought them into the mouth of the Delaware estuary three months later.

A formal "Instruction" was given to Printz before he left Sweden. Although it was not signed by Queen Christina, her name appears in it several times with the indication that she had read and endorsed what the men in control of the kingdom had decided. Christina was then in her seventeenth year; she was not proclaimed ruler until December 8, 1644, but she had been attending meetings of the Council of State, where, it is said, she volunteered her advice. The knowledge that she would soon occupy the throne obviously had an influence on the regents still running the country, who were well aware of her potential power as head of state. However, Chancellor Oxenstierna seems to have been less inclined than the others to allow her wishes to prevail when he disagreed. He was now sixty years of age and he had differences of opinion with the strong-willed, assertive young queen-to-be.

Evidently Printz wanted a time limit set on his term of service in New Sweden, and one of the paragraphs in the Instruction reads:

> Her Royal Majesty is also well satisfied that the said office of his governorship shall continue and exist for three years, and after their expiration, he, Johan Printz, shall be free to return hither again, after the necessary arrangement has been made for his successor or some substitute in this service.

The Instruction was an important policy document, carefully written and recorded in the Royal Copy Book in the Royal Archives in Stockholm. The first paragraph makes clear that the expressed aim of the expedition was for "confirming and strengthening the project thus begun in New Sweden." If any doubt existed about whether the administrations of Måns Kling and Peter Hollander Ridder were intended as the beginnings of a permanent settlement, the Instruction leaves no question that Printz's goal was full-scale colonization.

Printz was charged with setting up a political government and administering justice in the name of her Royal Majesty and the

Crown of Sweden. He was cautioned to uphold the dignity of
the Crown and to be mindful of the interests of the company in
the conservation of the land and the maintenance of the colony.
He was charged with settling controversial matters in accor-
dance with Swedish laws and adapting the "laudable customs,
habits and usages of this praiseworthy kingdom." In short, New
Sweden, politically and socially, should become an offshoot of
the homeland and owe fealty to the Crown. In order to strengthen
the Swedish military position Printz was authorized to select a
site for another fort on the South River that could better command the river against intruders than Fort Christina.

Printz was instructed to make certain that divine worship was
zealously performed according to the Augsburg Confession and
the ceremonies of the Swedish church and that all persons,
especially the young, be thoroughly instructed in Christian disciplines. However, any Dutch colonists living in New Sweden
under Swedish rule should not be disturbed in the free exercise
of their Reformed religion. That, incidentally, was in contrast to
the prejudice against Lutherans held by officials of the Dutch
West India Company in the New Netherland.

Swedish behavior to the English, the Dutch, and the Indians
were clearly stated. According to the Instruction there were then
sixty English, including men, women, and children, living on
the Varkens Kill. This is unconfirmed in English records and
may be an exaggeration. Since the lands they occupied were
within the boundaries of New Sweden, Printz was supposed to
bring them under Swedish jurisdiction. However, it would be
preferable and desirable to "get rid of them out of and away
from that place in a peaceable manner," and it was left to
Printz's discretion how that could be accomplished "with grace
and propriety." The Swedish government did not want the
English from New Haven to remain in the colony, but neither
did the regents want to disrupt the friendly relations then existing between Sweden and England.

The Instruction emphasized that English merchants from Virginia had already begun to trade at Fort Christina and that such
commerce should be continued because the products were bene-

ficial to the colony. The irony is apparent—Printz was supposed to shun the New Englanders but cultivate the friendship of the Virginians.

Objections to Swedish occupancy by officers of the Dutch West India Company should be refuted by insisting that the Swedes occupied land legally purchased from the Indians and that the Dutch had no right to interfere. The remonstrance was supposed to be made mildly, but should the Dutch show enmity, or make a hostile encroachment, Printz was to use his best discretion and repel force with force if necessary. With this caveat the Instruction went on to qualify that the only thing the Swedes sought was the retention of their property and a free exercise of commerce, and if the Dutch did not disturb them, Printz was told to maintain friendship with those at Fort Nassau and at New Amsterdam.

The Indians should be treated with all humanity and respect without wronging them or doing them violence. At every opportunity Printz should see that they were instructed in the true Christian religion and worship, and otherwise taught civilization "as though led by the hand." In bartering with the Indians he should offer trade goods at more moderate prices than either the Dutch or English offered so that the "said wild people may be withdrawn from them, and so much the more turn to our own people."

The Instruction further encouraged Printz to:

pay good and close attention to the cultivation of tobacco and appoint thereto a certain number of laborers, pressing the matter so that the cultivation may increase and more and more continued and extended, so that he can send over a good quantity of tobacco on all ships coming hither.

The Swedish officials continued to think of tobacco in the same terms as raising barley or rye, unaware that many factors entered into cultivating marketable American tobacco. Weather conditions, insect pests, fungi, transplanting the young plants to well-fertilized fields, and curing the leaves were all part of the process with which Swedish and Finnish farmers were unfamiliar. The natural tendency of Scandinavian farmers was to raise edible grains to feed their families as they had done in their homeland.

Printz was also directed to do his utmost to increase the quantity of furs sent to Sweden and to be vigilant that the fur trade was restricted to the New Sweden Company. At that time none of the freemen or other noncompany employees were permitted to barter with the Indians for furs.

In addition to raising tobacco and promoting the fur trade, the Instruction urged Printz to give attention to certain other products that were marketable in Sweden. Among those was wool. Printz was told to breed a good strain of sheep and to establish as many sheepfolds as possible. He was also requested to investigate whether or not metals or minerals could be found and if a salt works could be established on the seacoast to provide Sweden and Finland with salt then usually obtained from Spain and Portugal.

Other exportable products worthy of investigation were wine made from the wild grapes that were plentiful in New Sweden, lumber from oak and walnut trees, and oil pressed out of walnuts. Printz was also to determine whether profitable fisheries could be established, especially a whale fishery in the Delaware Bay, which was really a long shot. The Dutch patroons learned ten years before that the whales frequenting local waters yielded very little oil. Blommaert would have known all about the expensive fiasco undertaken by patroons a decade before, but his expert advice was no longer available to the Swedish government.

A final will-o-the-wisp that Printz was directed to investigate was the raising of silkworms to ascertain if Sweden could not develop an American silk industry to compete with Japan. No one in Sweden fully understood the delicate process involving moths of a certain species that lay their eggs in mulberry trees, where their larvae voraciously ate the leaves and then spun cocoons whose gossamer threads were gently unwound by deft female fingers. It would be difficult to think of a manufacture less adapted to horny-handed Swedes and Finns building log cabins and grubbing the soil for a living than sericulture.

Printz had plenty of time to read and reread the Instruction during the long and tedious voyage through the English Channel, south along the coast of Portugal, then to the Canary Islands, and across the Atlantic, taking advantage of winds blowing east to west. After a Christmas holiday in the hot tropical weather in Antigua, the two vessels sailed past Saint Christopher, Saint Bartholomew, and Saint Martin, according to a journal kept by Reverend Johan Campanius. They then proceeded northwest into the cold-weather zone reaching in late January the Delaware Bay, where they encountered a violent snowstorm that extensively damaged the sails and masts of both vessels. After a two-week delay in which temporary repairs were made, the battered vessels and their cold and frightened passengers made their way up the Delaware, swung into the mouth of the Minquas Kill, and landed at Fort Christina on February 15, 1643.

Among those who greeted the new arrivals at "the Rocks" were Peter Hollander Ridder, Lieutenant Måns Kling, Commissary Hendrick Huygen, and the Reverend Reorus Torkillus. They were all known to Gregorius van Dyck who had met them during his previous term of service at Fort Christina, and he was able to present them to Governor Printz and to introduce them to the Reverends Campanius and Fluviander. The soldiers stationed at the fort and the colonists living in the nearby cabins pressed forward for a view of the new governor and his family. Few had ever seen such a mountain of a man, and in a community where females were scarce the five Printz daughters must have aroused curiosity. The ages of the girls are not known, but one of them, presumably the oldest, Armegot, was mature enough for marriage.

Printz was not one to lose this golden moment to dramatize his propitious arrival after surviving a death-defying winter storm. He probably addressed the assemblage and left no doubt that he was the choice of God, Queen Christina, and the Council of State to rule the colony. He no doubt referred to the cargo of supplies he had brought from Sweden and to the additional ships that would shortly arrive to make him master of the river.

From the moment his heels clacked on the stoney wharf he was in full charge of New Sweden.

No one was happier to greet the new governor than Ridder. His assignment as governor had not been of his choosing, and three years service in an untamed land was long enough for a naval officer with a restless temperament. Two months later on April 14, 1643, when the *Fama* and the *Swan* left Fort Christina, he and several others, including Herr Christopher, returned to Sweden. When Ridder reached the homeland, Treasurer Johan Beier must have realized that Ridder had earned the salary owed to him for his dedicated service to the company and the Crown. The *Fama* and *Swan* were loaded down with a large cargo of beaver and otter skins that he had accumulated at Fort Christina during his administration, and, in addition, the vessels carried a consignment of salt picked up in Portugal enroute to Sweden. Ridder resumed his military service, and the government restored his lieutenancy. During the years that followed he was successively promoted in rank during a long and illustrious career in the admiralty.

Before the *Fama* and the *Swan* arrived back in Sweden, preparations were already being made to send Printz additional people and supplies, especially goods for use in the Indian trade. On the previous voyage there had not been time to accumulate trade merchandise in Holland, and the stores at Fort Christina used for barter were almost exhausted. In the absence of efficient land transportation and fast means of communication, preparations for ocean voyages were slow and laborious, often requiring months. Obtaining merchandise in the days before the developments of the so-called Industrial Revolution involved production in homes and small workshops, where much of the work was done by hand. After the time-consuming process of accumulating the goods at a port like Gothenburg, it was a major task to load it aboard a sailing vessel without causing an imbalance of the cargo after the ship set sail.

When the two vessels arrived, the *Fama* was selected to return to New Sweden alone, and high priority was given to refitting her and making her fully seaworthy for another hazardous crossing. The cargo contained a preponderance of Indian trade merchandise, including 250 copper kettles, much in demand by the natives. Printz badly needed the trade goods, not only to barter for beaver pelts but also for presents that it was necessary to give periodically to the Indian leaders to assure their continued friendship. The goods purchased in Amsterdam and Stockholm for use by the colonists included axes, three large saws for building a sawmill, stones for a gristmill, 200 pairs of stockings, 300 pairs of shoes, linens, 6,000 bricks, pitch, a ton of lime, 200 barrels of flour, ten hogsheads of French wine, clothing, and other commodities Printz had requisitioned.

In the haste to obtain trade goods in preparation for the sailing, there was insufficient time to organize a recruitment drive for colonists, which would have delayed the voyage. As a consequence there were very few passengers aboard when the *Fama* left port on December 29, 1643.

Lieutenant Johan Papegoja, who had previously been stationed at Fort Christina, returned on the vessel after hiring a number of soldiers to serve in the colony. They were all volunteers, except one—a soldier from Finland, discredited for unknown reasons, was condemned to permanent exile in America. Hans Janeke, the barber-surgeon, was again engaged and given sixty daler to prepare his medicine chest for general practice in New Sweden. Among the other passengers were two farmers from Finland proper, who were deported for having committed adultery, and two venturous young noblemen, Per and Knut Liljehok.

The *Fama* did not leave the port alone; the *Kalmar Nyckel* also departed at the same time. Her destination was the Caribbean, and she carried a cargo of brandy, wine, lumber, tar, wooden utensils, and other commodities that the company expected to dispose of in the islands and then load up with tobacco to meet the ever-growing demand in Sweden. The two ships held to the same course for a number of weeks, but they parted company after reaching American waters. The *Fama* continued on alone to Fort Christina.

When the *Fama* arrived on March 11, 1644, Printz was overjoyed at the quantity of trade goods that permitted him to renew traffic with the Indians. June was a good month to buy pelts. When the Fama was ready to head homeward on July 12, there were 2,142 beaver pelts in her hold, some large and some small, as well as a large consignment of cured tobacco leaves. Printz purchased most of the tobacco from the English in Virginia, but some had been grown by the Connecticut people on the Varkens Kill, and a small quantity by Swedes and Finns raised in the fields near Fort Christina. The current rate for Virginia tobacco was six or seven stuivers a pound, but to encourage the farmers in New Sweden to become more interested in raising tobacco he paid them eight stuivers a pound for their yield. He wrote that he had another ulterior motive; when the news reached Sweden that their countrymen were beginning to prosper in America it would encourage other farmers to come to the colony to seek their fortunes.

Like the other Swedish money used in the seventeenth century, it is impossible to estimate the value of a stuiver in modern terms. Whatever its value was, Printz seemed to think that eight stuivers a pound was an adequate incentive to arouse interest in tobacco farming in New Sweden. He may have overestimated the value of the tobacco, but it is certain that he overestimated the response of Swedish farmers. There was still no rush to New Sweden to raise tobacco, or anything else for that matter. Incidentally, the *Kalmar Nyckel* had a very profitable voyage to the Caribbean, safely returning home from Saint Christopher, where she had sold her cargo and taken aboard all the tobacco the vessel could carry. She was welcomed home with enthusiasm, and there was no problem in disposing of her cargo. The tobacco market was now booming in Sweden!

5. PRINTZ EXPANDS NEW SWEDEN

Before Peter Hollander Ridder returned to Sweden he accompanied Governor Printz on a tour of the territory south to Cape Henlopen and north to the Sankikans, and from Cape May on the east side of the bay up the river as far as Narraticon Creek. They undoubtedly went by boat, having soldiers and perhaps a Lenape guide in the party. The winter snows had melted and the exploration gave the new governor the overview of New Sweden necessary to execute the provisions in his Instruction. Printz sized up the lands that seemed best suited for agriculture, where new colonists could be assigned to build their houses and farms, and he examined prospective sites for a new fort that would dominate the Delaware River. Since Ridder originally made the suggestion of building a fort on the main river, we can assume that he shared his ideas with Printz. When Printz saw the actual topography and the extensive area comprising New Sweden, he realized that it would be necessary to build more than one new fort to safeguard the colony.

Printz made two significant decisions. First, he would build the major fort on the east side of the Delaware River diagonally southeast from present New Castle at or near the mouth of the Varkens Kill and call it Fort Elfsborg, the name of an imposing fortress at Gothenburg, Sweden. Second, he decided to move the "capital" of the colony from Fort Christina, where his predecessors Minuit, Kling, and Ridder had all lived, to an upriver island known to the Indians as Matinicum ("at the island'') but abbreviated by the Swedes to Tinicum.* The island lay along the west shore of the Delaware south of the mouth of the Schuylkill River not far distant from the present-day Philadelphia International Airport. He planned to build a second fort on Tinicum Island, and he selected a name before it was built—Fort New Gothenburg. Although the Instruction directed him to build one new fort, the phraseology could readily be construed to mean that it was within his authority to construct whatever defenses were required to meet the political and military needs of the colony. He also had a personal reason for selecting Tinicum Island; he decided to make his home there, and this, too, was within his authority according to the Instruction.

The Printz family was then temporarily living at Fort Christina, but as the chief administrator of the colony, Printz wanted a tract of land that he could call his own, where he could erect a commodious dwelling. He was apparently convinced that his aristocratic wife and five daughters deserved a gubernatorial mansion better suited to their needs than anything Fort Christina afforded. A man in his position with a dominantly female household needed a home environment where he could pick and choose their company without having them exposed to coarse farmers and soldiers, some of whom were illiterate. Printz does not explain in any of his letters why he selected Tinicum Island as a home site instead of one of many other suitable locations on the river, but obviously the fertile soil, the beauty of the natural setting, the privacy, and the proximity of the Delaware River were factors that appealed to him.

Printz sent with Ridder his request to the Council of State that the government officially grant him Tinicum Island as his own personal property. While awaiting a reply, he set about building Fort Elfsborg, which was intended as a fortress to prevent unfriendly vessels from ascending the river. He planned to give it sufficient firepower to block Dutch access to Fort Nassau if his superiors in Stockholm ordered him to do so. The fort was

---

*Not to be confused with Burlington Island, known to the Indians as Matinakonk.

also intended to assert authority over the English settlement on the Varkens Kill, and, if necessary, to prevent further incursions of New Englanders in the river.

Lieutenant Sven Skute, then second in authority to Printz, was given command of the fort; Gregorius van Dyck was named the head guard; Johann Matsson, a gunner; and Sven Andersson, a drummer. Because of his limited manpower Printz could spare only thirteen soldiers for the garrison of what was intended to be the strongest Swedish military post on the river. The records do not refer to wives or children at the fort, and the likelihood is that most of the soldiers were single, although some later married and lived elsewhere.

The Dutch navigator David de Vries piloted a Dutch fishing smack up the Delaware River in the fall of 1643, carrying a cargo of Madeira wine that the captain hoped to sell to the Swedes. The Swedish garrison at Fort Elfsborg forced the captain to strike his colors on October 13 when he came opposite the fort. The date is important because de Vries noted in his journal that the fort was then not entirely finished, but "it was made after the English plan with three angles close by the river." No drawing of the fort has been preserved, but the description seems to mean that three armed bastions were built overlooking the river, each having cannon aimed to deter vessels from passing. From another source we learn that Printz bought 2,700 feet of oak planks to be used in constructing the fort. When completed, Printz armed the port with the largest weapons in the colony—four iron and four brass cannon that fired twelve-pound balls, and one mortar, a smaller cannon with a short barrel. There is some question about the precise location of the fort, but it is believed to have been on an island on or near "Elsingburg Fort Point" in Elsinboro Township, Salem County. To the Swedes an island was not necessarily a land mass set in a body of water; the term could also describe a site on a major river separated from the mainland by a small tidal stream serving as a natural moat. In a property inventory Printz noted that the English had cleared and cultivated thirty morgens (approximately sixty acres) "in the environs of Fort Elfsborg," which suggests the English settlement was close to the fort.

Before Fort Elfsborg was completed, construction began at Fort New Gothenburg on Tinicum Island. This island also fronted on the Delaware River and was insular only because of a narrow creek on the west side separating it from the mainland. Tinicum Island has undergone many physical changes, but in Printz's time it was roughly triangular in shape, about one and one-half miles wide at its widest part and perhaps two miles long. The fort, built of squared hemlock logs laid horizontally one on the other in the shape of a blockhouse was on a high point near the water's edge. It was armed with four small copper cannon pointed toward the river. Initially the fort was manned by two gunners and eight soldiers. Near the creek on the land side Printz erected a storehouse that could also be used as a redoubt in the event of Indian attack by land.

When the *Fama* arrived again on March 11, 1644, she brought a patent dated November 6, 1643, granting Printz and his heirs "a capital donation at that place called Tinnaco or New Gothenburg." Printz received the first tract of land that the Swedish government granted to an individual owner; all other settlers in the colony—freemen, employes, and servants—were living on land considered to be either the property of the government or the New Sweden Company, although they lived rent-free and paid no land tax.

The mansion called Printzhoff ("Printz Hall"), erected on an elevation on Tinicum Island, was built of hewn logs two stories high. The interior was fitted with sawn lumber, and the fireplaces and chimneys were made of bricks brought on the *Fama*. The floors were probably made of hewn planks, and the house had an unusual feature—windows made of glass brought from Sweden on the *Fama*.* The estate also had gardens, an orchard, a summer house, and other structures not present on the properties occupied by ordinary Finnish and Swedish settlers. One of

---

*The house was destroyed by fire in 1645 but was rebuilt more spaciously than before.

MAINLAND

THE DITCH

DELAWARE RIVER

THE AUTHOR'S CONCEPT OF

TINICUM ISLAND

GOVERNOR PRINTZ'S SLOOP

THE "CAPITAL" OF NEW SWEDEN FROM 1644 TO 1654

GOVERNOR PRINTZ'S LAND WAS CULTIVATED AND HIS 50 BEASTS WERE HORSES AND COWS. AND SHEEP.

"Twelve morgans of field, fifty beasts and the buildings which belong to Governor Printz" - [VALUE 4,000 R.D. - RIKSDALAR]

(12 MORGANS = 24 ACRES

FORT NEW GOTHENBURG
4 CANNON FACING RIVER

ROCKS INSIDE A
BADSTU   BADSTU WITH FIRE BOX

"PRINTZHOFF"
CLAPBOARD ROOF AND GLASS WINDOWS

BELL TOWER

LOG CHURCH AND CEMETERY
- N. SAWIN ©

the buildings known as a *badstu* was where the family took sweat baths, an old Scandinavian custom.

The public records of the colony were kept at Printzhoff, including Indian deeds, salary rolls of officers and soldiers, and other private and official documents, including the minutes of the court when cases were tried there. One writer noted that since Tinicum Island later became part of Pennsylvania Printzhoff could be considered the first statehouse of the commonwealth. The island was assuredly the political "capital" of New Sweden and a new center of authority during Printz's administration, but to relate it to the government of Pennsylvania is a little premature. The year Printzhoff was built, William Penn was born in London, and he did not found Pennsylvania until thirty-eight years later.

Printz's accomplishments in New Sweden were truly remarkable considering the odds against him. The illness that caused the death of Pastor Torkillus may have been undernourishment, because twelve laborers, eight soldiers, two freemen, and two women died shortly thereafter. Limited manpower was serious, but it was not the only problem.

Misunderstandings developed with the Lenape, and in his first report to the New Sweden Company, dated June 11, 1644, Printz stated that the Indians "murdered a man and wife in their bed, and a few days afterwards they killed two soldiers and a workman." It is difficult to reconcile those acts with the belief that relations between Lenape and Swedes were always friendly. Following those murders Printz summoned the Lenape chiefs to Fort Christina to negotiate a peace treaty. In the report of 1644 he said that he told the chiefs:

> that in case they hereafter practised the smallest hostilities against our people then we would not let a soul of them live, upon which they gave their writing and all their sachems signed their names to it and (according to their custom) gave us twenty beavers [pelts] and some sewant and we presented them with a piece of cloth in return. But yet they do not trust us and we trust them less.

Printz was not impressed with the Lenape from the time of

his arrival. In a personal letter to Chancellor Oxenstierna dated April 14, 1643, he referred to them as "deceitful, vindictive, anger-harboring and hasty." He repeated a number of times in his letters and reports that he would like to get rid of the Lenape because they had few beaver pelts to trade in contrast with the abundance of beaver pelts available from the Minquas. Printz had a much higher regard for the Minquas than he had for the Lenape, although when food was scarce he was glad to buy corn from the latter, who cultivated extensive fields near their villages.

Although the Lenape were not warlike people they reacted to mistreatment or abuse, and because they greatly outnumbered the Swedes Printz was always apprehensive of an Indian attack. The Dutch in New Amsterdam lost many settlers in wars with the Indians, and Printz heard rumors that the Indians in Virginia had banded together and killed 600 Christians. He was aware that New Sweden could not survive a major Indian attack and that he did not have enough soldiers to defend the colony against a foreign invasion. He reported to Sweden that if he were reinforced with soldiers and good officers "then with the help of God not a single savage would be allowed to live on this River." Although adequate reinforcements were never sent to him, he nevertheless continued undaunted in his expansion plans as though he had an invincible army at his command.

Printz's building program included renovating Fort Christina, which he repaired from top to bottom because it was so badly decayed. After strengthening the fort he could spare only a handful of soldiers for the garrison, but he placed Lieutenant Johan Papegoja in command as though the lieutenant had a full regiment in reserve. Actually there were now only two strong subordinates in Papegoja's command, Hendrick Huygen, who continued to hold the post of commissary, and Huygen's young cousin Gotfried Harmer, who developed a proficiency in the Indian languages and often acted as the official interpreter.

Papegoja became enamored of Armegot Printz, and he asked the Reverend Campanius to intercede for him with Printz for his daughter's hand. Printz, for unknown reasons, was reluctant to consent, and Papegoja wrote a letter to the esteemed Count Per

Brahe, a member of the Council of State, asking that he exert his influence on Printz. "If one were in Sweden," he wrote, "there would be no want; but here one must himself cook and bake and himself do all the things that women do, which I am not accustomed to, and it is difficult for me." Brahe wrote Printz recommending Papegoja, stating that the young man had the Count's confidence. Printz ultimately relented and consented to the marriage.

The building of Fort New Gothenburg and the movement of the Printz family to Tinicum Island, with Printz's headquarters at Printzhoff, changed the economic landscape of the colony. Although Fort Christina continued to be an important post in the Minquas trade and its usefulness as a port in the coastal commerce did not diminish, a number of Swedish and Finnish families moved north to settle on the upriver tributaries to the Delaware. Servants of the Printz family and members of his staff built cabins on Tinicum Island, and some farmed the land.

Printz erected a log blockhouse on the river shore at a place known to the Lenape as Mechopinackan about two miles south of Tinicum, which was called Upland (present Chester) after a Swedish province. Some of the Swedes who settled there may have come from Upland. An area at Upland extending south to present-day Marcus Hook, called Chamassung by the Indians, became known as Finland because of the number of Finnish families who settled there.

Printz built a blockhouse called Nya Vasa (Vasa was a city in Finland) on a creek at a place called Kingsessing, and several farm families built cabins in the vicinity. That area was important in the beaver trade because Nya Vasa was on the Minquas trail that led to the Conestoga and Susquehanna rivers.

Printz built another blockhouse called New Korsholm ("Cross Island") on an island west of the mouth of the Schuylkill, described as "a fine little fort of logs, having sand and stone filled in between the woodwork and surrounded by palisades." Lieutenant Måns Kling was stationed there initially, after Papegoja replaced him at Fort Christina, and several freemen and servants built dwellings nearby as time went on.

The windmill at Fort Christina, the only gristmill in the colony, in charge of Anders Kristiansson Dreijer, did not satisfy Printz. He wrote that it "would never work and was good for nothing," which was probably an exaggeration, although it had the obvious disadvantage of being operative only when the wind was blowing. Deprived of dependable milling facilities, the families had to pound their own wheat and corn into flour and cornmeal in hand mills. As a replacement for the windmill, Printz erected the first water-powered gristmill in the colony in 1646 at a place on the east side of Cobbs Creek known to the Indians as Kakarikong (Karakong, Carcoens), which the Swedes renamed Mölndal ("the flour valley") after a place in Sweden. The site of the mill was above the present-day Woodland Avenue Bridge that crosses Cobbs Creek in Philadelphia.

The mill was of an ancient type called a "Norse mill," a one-room log structure built directly over the little stream. A vertical wooden shaft, the lower end fitted with blades or paddles, turned as the force of the flowing water caused it to revolve. The upper end of the shaft passed through two circular millstones placed in the floor of the structure, one on top of the other. The lower stone was stationary, but the upper one was fastened to the shaft and revolved as the shaft turned. The grain was ground between the surface of the two stones, its fineness depending upon increasing or decreasing the space between the two stones. A wooden hopper controlled by hand regulated the quantity of grain fed to the millstones. It was doubtless a "custom mill," which means customers brought their own grain and paid the miller a portion of the flour he ground for them.

The Colonial Dames of America purchased an old Norse mill in Sweden and erected it on the site of the Cobbs Creek mill with suitable dedicatory services in 1926. The mill was actually put in operation and became a popular tourist attraction. Unfortunately it was washed away in a flood in 1928.

To the extent that his limited manpower and other handicaps permitted, Printz did his best to comply with his Instruction. Although the Swedish and Finnish farmers would have preferred to raise corn rather than tobacco because it entailed much less

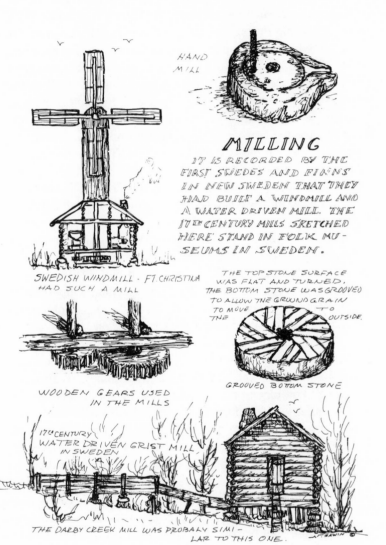

HAND MILL

MILLING

IT IS RECORDED BY THE FIRST SWEDES AND FINNS IN NEW SWEDEN THAT THEY HAD BUILT A WINDMILL AND A WATER DRIVEN MILL. THE 17ᵀᴴ CENTURY MILLS SKETCHED HERE STAND IN FOLK MUSEUMS IN SWEDEN.

SWEDISH WINDMILL - FT. CHRISTINA HAD SUCH A MILL

THE TOP STONE SURFACE WAS FLAT AND TURNED. THE BOTTOM STONE WAS GROOVED TO ALLOW THE GROUND GRAIN TO MOVE TO THE OUTSIDE.

GROOVED BOTTOM STONE

WOODEN GEARS USED IN THE MILLS

17ᵀᴴ CENTURY WATER DRIVEN GRIST MILL IN SWEDEN

THE DARBY CREEK MILL WAS PROBABLY SIMILAR TO THIS ONE.

work, Printz arranged to buy corn from the Lenape and ordered the farmers to turn their cornfields into tobacco "plantations." Three reasonably large tobacco plantations were laid out, as were several smaller ones. The largest one was at Upland, where twelve men were engaged under the direction of an expert planter, possibly an Englishman who had worked in the tobacco fields of Virginia. One of the Swedish tobacco planters at Upland was Johan Andersson Stålkofta, whose name will later reappear in this volume.

The second largest tobacco plantation was in the vicinity of Fort Christina, where eleven tobacco planters worked in the fields, and the third largest was on the Schuylkill, possibly on the island where Lieutenant Kling was stationed. Seven planters were employed at the latter site.

Printz had several good carpenters, who built two new boats and repaired the two sloops that had been in the colony for a number of years. One of the carpenters, a skilled workman, built two excellent wooden "gates" or defensive portals for Fort Elfsborg and Fort New Gothenburg. The carpenters also built a wharf in the river near Fort Christina, which appears to have been a place of boat manufacture as well as a dock, and two coopers also worked there making barrels, tubs, wooden milk pails, tobacco casks, and the like. There were also two blacksmith shops in operation, one at Fort Christina and the other at Upland. Of course, Printz also encouraged the cultivation of rye and barley, and he purchased seven oxen and a cow from the Dutch at New Amsterdam. Careful attention was given to taking care of the several horses, cattle, swine, and sheep in the colony. All of the improvements just discussed did not occur overnight; they were attained over a period of three or four years. There seems little question, though, that Printz must have been a hard taskmaster to accomplish what he did with so few workmen and the limited supplies at his disposal.

It is not difficult to understand why some of the desired objectives were not attained. Time did not permit whaling or salt-making, and it quickly became apparent that the weather was not conducive to raising silkworms. Printz did not find the gold mine that the Dutch claimed lay between New Sweden and New Amsterdam, nor did he ever see any of the gold reportedly found there. Nevertheless, through his leadership Printz accomplished more than any of his predecessors in expanding the colony, despite the fact that many of the people didn't enjoy life in New Sweden and wanted to return home. This was a ticklish situation because the freemen who went to America to better their fortunes were promised the liberty of returning home when they pleased, but if they left it encouraged the desertion of employees, soldiers, and servants, all of whom were under obligation to the company to remain for stated periods of time.

On September 4, 1646, the Reverend Campanius consecrated a new Lutheran church, built of logs with a roof of clapboards bought from the English, on the southwest point of Tinicum Island. The church with its adjacent graveyard became the religious center for the upriver Swedes and Finns, and some parishioners came at times from as far as Fort Christina. The Reverend Campanius married Lieutenant Papegoja and Armegot Printz in this little church, no doubt a gala day in the colony.

In Sweden a wedding was primarily a religious function, although numerous social traditions were observed when the families of the couple discussed the possibility of marriage. Parents and older relatives decided whether the match was suitable, and if they came to agreement during their discussions, which involved both families, a dowry was negotiated. A period of discreet courtship preceded the marriage, and banns were proclaimed on three successive Sundays by the minister before a wedding date was set. There is no record of the customs that were observed in the Printz household when the governor and his wife consented to Armegot's betrothal, but the Printz family belonged to the upper class and doubtless conformed to the mores of their social position as far as possible. The absence of Papegoja's family obviously required changes in the procedure, and living conditions were far different in New Sweden from those in Printz's home in Bottnaryd in the province of Smaland.

Nevertheless, there was probably a betrothal ceremony where Armegot and Papegoja exchanged presents and then a sumptuous meal was served. In Sweden the betrothal dinner was always followed by dancing, and it seems safe to speculate that there was some kind of dancing after the betrothal ceremony at Printzhoff, and at the wedding, which usually occurred six months to a year after the betrothal. The question arises about the kind of betrothal and wedding music that accompanied the dancers, but it must remain unanswered since the New Sweden records contain no information about instrumentalists in the colony other than those assigned to the military. Erick Andersson came with Printz's soldiers as a trumpeter, and Sven Andersson was a drummer. A later reference to "a pipe" suggests a flutist may have contributed to martial music, but a drum, a trumpet, and a flute are scarcely suitable for dancing.

In Sweden the male friends of the groom usually held a bachelor's party, and the bride was entertained by female friends on a "maiden's evening," where "maiden porridge" was the chief dish. The porridge contained an almond, and the girl who got the serving with the hidden nut was supposed to be the next one to be married. There were enough unmarried men in New Sweden to warrant a bachelor's party, but the marriageable maidens may have been too scarce for a "maiden's evening," so perhaps married women attended.

A wedding banquet at the bride's house usually followed the church ceremony. The menu for a wedding banquet consisted of a dozen courses interspersed with generous portions of brandy and beer. Musicians played during the banquet, and after the meal, tables were removed for dancing, including a "farewell dance" where the bride danced with all the single male guests and the groom with the unmarried girls. Finally the groom danced with the bride, and the whole party, led by the musicians, filed into the bridal chamber with the married couple. In full view of all the guests the bride and groom got into the bed—fully clothed. After a while they were left alone as the guests departed. The day after the wedding was spent in merrymaking, eating, and dancing, and on the third or fourth day the married couple moved to their new home. Their belongings were put in order to receive guests, and after more refreshments and dancing the wedding festivities were over.

Papegoja and Armegot moved to one of the houses erected by the company at Fort Christina. Their marriage was blessed with five children, three boys and two girls. In time, though, the marriage turned into an unhappy union, and the couple periodically separated. Armegot seems to have preferred living in America, whereas Papegoja returned to his estate in Sweden and became a captain in the Swedish navy. After her father returned to Sweden she moved back to Printzhoff, where she lived as a grand dame until 1662, when she sold Tinicum Island to a Dutchman for 6,000 guilders "as attorney for her father." Printz, then living in Sweden, died the following year, 1663.

Armegot's attachment to Tinicum Island seems to have been shared by many of the Swedish and Finnish families who settled in the immediate vicinity. Even those who lived at some distance attended church services by boat, the rivers and creeks serving as highways before the Indian paths were widened into passable roads. By erecting a church on the island Printz not only complied with his Instruction to "see to it that to God and the most High be paid in all things a true and befitting worship," he also gave the colony a strong spiritual bond. Such cohesiveness gave the Scandinavian people a separate identity that lasted for many years after the fall of New Sweden.

The Reverend Johan Campanius was a dedicated pastor who did his utmost to assist Printz in attaining one of the goals in his Instruction, namely to convert the Indians to Christianity. As Torkillus's successor (he conducted the funeral rites for his predecessor at Fort Christina), he held services regularly in the chapel. After the church was built on Tinicum Island he was in charge of conducting services there. Campanius had studied theology at the University of Uppsala, after which he served in Russia as a chaplain in the Swedish legation. Following his return from Russia he was employed as a schoolmaster in a small town north of Stockholm and was later appointed resident clergyman at the orphan's home in Stockholm. He was forty-one years of age when he accepted Admiral Fleming's invitation to go to New Sweden. It is known that a son Johan accompanied him on his mission, but it is uncertain if his wife was with him or any of his other children, believed to have numbered a total of seven. There are reasons to infer from a letter he wrote in New Sweden that some of his children, and perhaps his wife, remained in Sweden. Campanius had a farm at Upland, and a record of his selling a calf to another Swede suggests that he raised a few cattle.

Campanius was the first Swede, and, in fact, one of the earliest Europeans, to give serious study to the customs and languages of the Indians in the Middle Atlantic states. Only a few of his contemporaries, like Hendrick Huygen, Gotfried Harmer, Jacob Svensson, and Gregorius van Dyck, made an effort to learn enough of the Indian dialect to be able to converse with them in a kind of jargon when bartering for furs. Since many of the Swedes and Finns could not read or write their own language it is not surprising that little interest was shown in Indian linguistics and the etymological differences between the Lenape and Minquas tongues. Campanius deliberately set about familiarizing himself with Indian words and native idioms, keeping careful notes. He was, of course, handicapped by the absence of a written vocabulary or grammar to which he could refer, and he recorded the sounds of the Indian words in the letters of the Swedish alphabet. One had to be familiar with the pronunciation of the Swedish characters in order to read a word that an Indian would understand.

Campanius began a tour of the Indian communities, and at the end of two years he could communicate in both the Lenape and Minquas dialects. His governing motive was to teach the Indians about Jesus Christ in their own language. The Creator, or Great Spirit, in the Lenape religion had his parallel in the God of Lutheran tenets, and this concept the Indians could understand. Dreams and visions were part of the native religious pattern, and this helped Campanius to make them understand the dreams and visions experienced by Biblical characters. Of course, the Indian ceremonies, feasts, dances, and religious rites differed from Christian teaching, and Campanius had no doubt they were heathens from the viewpoint of Lutheran disciplines. Although Governor Printz encouraged Campanius's missionary work, he had little hope of success. He wrote that "when we speak to them about God they pay no attention, but they will let it be understood that they are a free people, subject to no one, but do what they please. I presume it would be possible to convert them, but only with great labor."

Nevertheless, Campanius persisted in his efforts although he had a busy schedule accommodating his Swedish parishioners and providing food and clothing for his family. Printz insisted upon the pastor wearing a chausable and conducting services as in Sweden, which included "solemn prayer days, Sundays and Apostle days . . . on Fridays and Wednesdays, sermons, and on all other days prayers, evening and morning." After 1647 when Fluviander left the colony, Campanius was the only remaining pastor, and Printz appointed literate laymen to conduct evening and morning prayers in the scattered communities for those unable to attend services at the church on Tinicum Island.

The keystone of Lutheranism was the catechism used principally to prepare children for their Christian confirmation, and to Campanius this seemed to be an indispensable religious tool in his missionary work among the Lenape, who were like children in religious matters. He commenced a task requiring painstaking effort—the translation of Martin Luther's *Little Catechism* into the Lenape dialect. In 1646 the manuscript was completed. He then began an evangelical tour of the Indian towns, calling forth the natives to listen to the words the Great Spirit had prepared for him to read to them.

Campanius was the first European scholar to record a religious tract into the Lenape tongue. An Indian Bible, published by the New England missionary John Eliot in 1664, is generally accepted as the first translation in the Indian language. When Eliot began his missionary work among the Indians in 1646, Campanius had already been working among the Lenape for three years. In 1656, eight years before Eliot's Bible was published, Campanius (who returned to Sweden on the *Swan* in

1648) presented his catechism to King Charles X of Sweden, although it was not published until 1696. The published catechism was used by some Swedish evangelists who followed Campanius to the New World. As an addendum to the catechism, Campanius added vocabularies in the Lenape and Minquas dialects. He also recorded notes on the customs of the Indians and kept a day-by-day journal of his weather observations for the year 1644. After his death this information was published in Sweden in 1702 by his grandson, Thomas Campanius Holm.

It cannot be said that Campanius encountered success as a missionary. Although his grandson wrote that he converted many Indians, there is no record of the names of any of them. The mission was not a happy or satisfying one for him, and he grew weary and requested his recall. In a letter written to his archbishop on January 30, 1647, he said he was well up in years, poor in health, and in need of a less arduous post in Sweden "which could support him with his wife and numerous little children." He stressed that he had been out of Sweden almost five years "with great danger of death night and day in a heathenish country, amongst these ferocious pagans, who for every year have threatened to slay us completely." Thomas Campanius Holm's book does not reveal his grandfather's deep frustrations.

From the time the *Fama* left New Sweden on her second voyage on June 20, 1644, Printz received no letters or supplies from Sweden until two years and four months later. On October 1, 1646, the *Gyllene Haj* (*Golden Shark*), usually abbreviated to the *Haj*, arrived at Fort Christina. It had been an interminably long wait for Printz. He was especially in need of trade goods to buy beaver pelts from the Minquas and to make gifts to the Lenape sachems. He also expected new colonists and the much-needed supplies he had requested. After the *Haj* arrived he learned from her captain that events in northern Europe, of greater concern to the welfare of Sweden than the colony on the Delaware, had commanded attention in Stockholm. Sweden and Denmark were again at war, and every ship that Admiral

LUTHERAN CHURCH FRÖSTHULT, SWEDEN — BUILT 1300 A.D., REMODELLED IN 1685. JOHAN CAMPANIUS PREACHED HERE FOR 32 YEARS AFTER RETURNING FROM AMERICA. HE DIED IN 1683, AGED 82 YEARS, AND IS BURIED UNDER THE FLOOR OF THE CHURCH WITH HIS WIFE, MARGARETA, WHO DIED IN 1682, AGED 72. THE CHURCH IS STILL STANDING, NOW ENLARGED WITH A TOWER AND BELFRY. (INFORMATION FROM PASTOR FRANK BLOMFELT.)

CAMPANIUS'S GRAVESTONE INSCRIBED IN LATIN, ALSO CONTAINS AN EPITAPH IN THE LENAPE DIALECT WRITTEN BY HIM, PROBABLY THE ONLY GRAVESTONE IN EUROPE WITH AN INDIAN INSCRIPTION.

"UMAR SACHIMAN CHINSIKKA HACKING HARO ANKAROP MACHIS CHUKI"

LENAPE SPEAKERS IN OKLAHOMA INTERVIEWED BY LINGUIST, JAMES A. REMENTER, SAY WORDS ARE A JARGON, NOT PURE LENAPE, WHICH SEEM TO MEAN:
"THE OLD PRIEST DIED AND IS BURIED HERE"

TITLE PAGE OF MARTIN LUTHER'S **LITTLE CATECHISM** IN LENAPE DIALECT BY CAMPANIUS, PUBLISHED IN 1696 IN STOCKHOLM

LUTHERI Catechismus/ öfwersatt på American-Virginiske Språket.

Stockholm/
Tryckt vthi thet af Sonst Monprivileg
BURCHARD·I·Amtervöl 3te Qnath 4
ANNO M DC XCVI.

N. SAWIN ©

CAMPANIUS PREACHING TO THE INDIANS IN THEIR OWN LANGUAGE.

Fleming could use was pressed into service. Even the *Fama* and *Kalmar Nyckel* were fitted out for military duty. No ships could be spared for voyages to America; the war absorbed all the attention of the government. The war not only delayed preparations for supplying Printz, it also cost the colony its most active supporter, for Admiral Fleming was killed in battle.

If Fleming had lived, the colony may not have been so badly neglected as it was when the over-burdened Chancellor Oxenstierna became the unappointed director of the New Sweden Company. The Danish war occupied nearly all of his attention. Oxenstierna wrote that he not only had to fight against the enemy but also against members of a peace party on the Council of State who opposed the war. Baron Spiring, then living in Holland, sent documents and reports received from Printz to Oxenstierna, but the Chancellor was too busy to look after them or meet for discussions with other officers of the company to keep them informed about conditions in New Sweden.

On August 13, 1645, peace terms with Denmark were negotiated, after which Sweden could spare vessels for commercial voyages. Although plans were made initially for a large expedition to support Printz, sufficient capital could not be raised. The *Haj* made the voyage alone when she weighed anchor in May of 1646. Her cargo included 5,835 yards of duffel cloth, 200 adzes, more than 100 pounds of "corals" (beads), 397 axes, 302 (copper?) kettles, 774 knives, 432 thimbles, 29 tin mugs, 144 tin pots, 504 horn combs, 264 knives, 10,000 fish-hooks, and a quantity of silver-plated and copper-plated ornamental chains, English caps, and many other articles used in the Indian trade. Valuable cargo space was required to transport that merchandise, and the *Haj* could not carry everything that Printz wanted, although some goods he requisitioned were sent, such as stockings, clothing, and hardware made in Nuremberg, Germany. The ship also carried wood planks needed for buildings since there was still no one able to build a sawmill in the colony. Some passengers were also taken aboard, although no special efforts were made to muster colonists for the voyage. The lack of people turned out for the best because the *Haj* was enroute for four miserable months, fighting ocean storms encountered on the voyage that carried away her topmasts, sails, and ruined some of the cargo.

Printz wrote that when the *Haj* arrived at Fort Christina most of the crew and passengers were ill, including the captain and first mate, and "would have despaired, had they not reached land when they did." The vessel was not completely repaired until December, and a severe winter that brought ice to the river delayed her return to Sweden until March of 1647. During the time the vessel was in dock under repair she was obviously out of commission and unproductive, a factor that had to be considered in the cost of the voyage.

Printz arranged with the captain of the *Haj* to take back a large cargo of tobacco he had accumulated weighing 24,177 Swedish pounds and filling 101 casks. Only 29 percent of the total quantity was raised in New Sweden—71 percent of the shipment was purchased from Dutch or English merchants. When the shipment arrived in Sweden the tobacco was valued at 4,000 Riksdaler, a substantial sum, but not sufficient to pay for the voyage. No pelts were delivered by the *Haj* to augment the cash return, because Printz's inventory of trade goods had long been exhausted, and he estimated he had lost 8,000 to 9,000 beaver pelts to the Dutch, who renewed their activity with the Minquas. The *Haj* had to depart before the trade goods she brought could be bartered in the late spring.

Printz did not wait for the Minquas to come to Sweden, because he wanted to compensate for the loss of pelts to the Dutch. He dispatched Hendrick Huygen, Gregorius van Dyck, and eight soldiers to carry presents to the Minquas in their own country and make arrangements to restore the trade by offering to pay more than the Dutch paid. It was a long trip of perhaps 100 or 150 miles each way because Huygen and van Dyck had to renew contacts at a number of Minquas villages. Printz's strategy was a success—the men returned with a quantity of beaver pelts and the promise of the Minquas chiefs to resume their business with the Swedes. Naturally the local Lenape chiefs, who were well aware of the Swedish mission to the

Minquas country, resented the negotiations with an enemy tribe. They wanted European goods, too, even though they had fewer beaver pelts to trade, and Printz reluctantly had to give presents to the Lenape chiefs to maintain the peace.

The Reverend Fluviander returned home on the *Haj* in the company of Lieutenant Papegoja, who went to Stockholm as an emissary carrying a written report from Printz with a long list of Printz's needs. The list included a bricklayer, a potter, a cooper, a locksmith, a blacksmith, and additional carpenters and laborers. Printz also made a plea that unmarried women be sent as prospective wives for the unmarried freemen. He requested more cannon and ammunition and complained that Dutch traders were bartering muskets, shot, and powder to the Indians, thus violating a gentlemen's agreement among the Europeans not to supply the natives with firearms. Regulations were enacted in the Dutch and English colonies to prevent such traffic, but as the natives became more sophisticated and demanded guns in exchange for furs the traders flagrantly violated the laws.

In early January of the following year (1648) Papegoja returned to Fort Christina on the *Swan*. The *Swan* left Gothenburg on September 25, 1647, bringing some of the merchandise Printz had requested, but there were only a few colonists and artisans aboard and no unmarried women. One of the passengers was a Lutheran pastor, the Reverend Lars Karlsson Lock, sent to replace Campanius. His name is variously spelled in the New Sweden records, e.g., Laurentius Carolus Lockenius, Lars Lock, Lars Carlsson Lock, Pastor Lock, etc., and he turned out to be an unruly character.

Campanius was more than willing to board the *Swan* when the vessel departed on May 16, and a number of people returned with her, one of whom was Lieutenant Måns Kling. He took back the journals and the salary and account books from February 1643 until March 1648. The chief bookkeeper Hans Kramer was obliged to audit the accounts and copy the figures in the company's official books. After completing his calculations, and making an inventory of the company's assets and liabilities, including the value of 1,232 beaver pelts and 64 otter skins Printz sent back on the *Swan*, he reported the finances were not in good condition; in fact, the annual balance showed a deficit.

Kramer lacked the gift of prophecy, and he did not understand what it meant to invest in the future. He had no way of knowing that the 13,000 square miles drained by the Delaware estuary would some day be occupied by 7.5 million people living in metropolitan Philadelphia, Camden, Trenton, Chester, Wilmington, and numerous smaller cities and towns occupying real estate of inestimable value. His main concern was to pay the bills and still have a sufficient balance to keep the company solvent, and that was a trying task.

6. TROUBLE WITH THE DUTCH

It was inevitable that Governor Printz's expansion of New Sweden would result in a clash with the Dutch. In complying with his Instruction he not only settled territory claimed by a rival nation, he also erected forts intended to command the Delaware River. Then as if to add insult to injury he used the fortified posts he erected on tributaries to the Delaware as bases to monopolize the fur business by over bidding Dutch traders.

Shortly after he arrived in New Sweden, Printz met Governor Willem Kieft, and Kieft perfunctorarily warned him that he was trespassing on Dutch territory, just as he had protested to Minuit when Fort Christina was under construction and then later to Minuit's successor, Ridder. Printz responded that both Minuit and Ridder had purchased the land from the rightful Indian owners, and he had no intention of vacating territory that was legally possessed by Queen Christina. Kieft knew that he did not have the authority to remove the Swedes physically, nor could he spare the soldiers to take military action on the Delaware even if he wanted to do so. As events developed, Kieft found a common interest with Printz in preventing the English from getting a foothold in the Delaware valley. Kieft was even more aware of the threat than was Printz because he had seen how the English moved into the Connecticut valley, becoming a military threat on the northern perimeter of New Netherland and an economic threat to the Dutch fur trade.

Kieft had another serious problem: due to his rash policies, hostility developed between the Dutch and the Indian tribes of upper New Jersey and the lower Hudson valley. All things considered, it seemed to him that co-existence with the Swedes would be the best course to follow. The forts Printz built provided a deterrent against English intrusion, and this served the common interest of the Dutch and the Swedes. Ridder cooperated with Kieft in the summer of 1642 when the Dutch burnt the English settlement on the Schuylkill and carried away the English settlers, but there was always the chance that the English might try again and with greater strength. Kieft recognized that Printz's forts would make it very difficult for the English to sail that far up the river again. The garrison at Fort Elfsborg could compel incoming vessels to drop anchor for boarding and inspection.

Kieft knew that Printz allowed English vessels from Virginia to sail up the river because they brought needed supplies to the Swedes without trying to make a settlement. The threat of colonization came from New England, and Printz allowed entry only to merchant ships from Boston or New Haven whose captains desired to do business with him. He could turn away those suspected of carrying colonists or trading with the Indians. Kieft could also detain vessels from New England enroute to the Delaware as they came into the harbor at New Amsterdam if he suspected their mission, and by doing so he was able to support Printz.

The English threat was an important factor in the development of a good rapport between the two governors, and there were even times when Swedish sloops picked up supplies in New Amsterdam with Kieft's approval. Kieft kept the lines of communication open between New Amsterdam and Printzhoff, often informing the Swedish governor about events taking place in Europe from the news passed on to him by Dutch skippers.

Printz reciprocated by doing nothing to molest the Dutch garrison at Fort Nassau, and as long as the Dutch did not attempt to settle on the west side of the Delaware, or build forts there, he tolerated the competition in the fur trade. The two governors appear to have had a healthy respect for each other, and in one of his reports Printz wrote that they enjoyed "unity and good friendship."

Kieft evidently got along better with Printz than he did with his own people in New Amsterdam. He was of patrician descent, an intelligent and cultured gentleman out of place in the milieu of New Netherland and unable to cope with the troubles that erupted during his administration. The Indian war solidified opposition to him. After seeing houses and barns go up in smoke and Dutch families massacred, Kieft ordered reprisal raids that caused a needless blood bath by inflicting unspeakable atrocities on Indian women and children. As a consequence of his mismanagement the directors of the West India Company recalled him, although he never reached Holland because the ship on which he was a passenger was wrecked, and Kieft drowned.

Kieft's successor was the legendary Peter Stuyvesant, who arrived at New Amsterdam with his wife on May 11, 1647. Stuyvesant had served the West India Company well in Brazil, earning a promotion to director of Dutch possessions in the Caribbean with his headquarters in Curaçao. His right foot was mangled by a Spanish cannon ball during a siege on the island of Saint Martin. After convalescing in Holland he arrived in New Netherland as the new director-general, limping on a silver-banded peg leg. The new post was his country's reward for faithful and meritorious service as a soldier and administrator. In his new job he was not only responsible for the government, commerce, and administration of civil and criminal law in New Netherland, he was also in charge of governing the "islands Curaçao, Buenaire [Bonaire], Aruba, and their dependencies." Those Dutch possessions in the West Indies were also under the supervision of the directors of the Amsterdam Chamber of the Company. It was an important and difficult assignment for a relatively young man. Recent research has shown that Stuyvesant was only thirty-six or thirty-seven years of age when he came to America. He was energetic, conscientious, well experienced in military affairs, and prudent in diplomacy. He was not then the elderly despot pictured in American folklore.

Stuyvesant and his Swedish counterpart, Johan Printz, were alike in many ways. Both were minister's sons and deeply religious men. Both had hot tempers and strong prejudices. As former army officers both had been conditioned by military disciplines to have their orders obeyed without question. Both men were dedicated to their jobs, although Stuyvesant may have been more highly principled than Printz. Stuyvesant was incorruptible and willing to sacrifice his personal interests for the benefit of his country. Printz allowed self-interest to creep into his administration, taking advantage of his position to accumulate wealth by conducting personal trade with the Indians and the English.

After Stuyvesant's arrival the long-smouldering differences between Swedes and Dutch over ownership of the land burst into flames. The conflagration occurred not at Fort Christina, but almost thirty miles north in the watershed of the Schuylkill River, where a number of Swedish and Finnish families had settled on New Sweden's northern frontier.

One of the Dutchmen who contributed to the discord that developed between Dutch and Swedes was an employee of the West India Company named Andries Hudde. A well-educated man, he was working as a surveyor in New Amsterdam when Governor Kieft transferred him to Fort Nassau to serve as the acting commander. He arrived at his new post on November 1, 1645, and after looking over the situation he immediately recognized that although the forts Printz built on the Delaware River prevented English incursions, the smaller trading posts west of the main river blocked the Dutch fur trade. Furthermore, a number of Swedish and Finnish colonists laid out their farms near the trading posts in the territory drained by the Schuylkill's tributaries. That enabled the Swedes to dominate the Minquas trade, as long as Printz had goods to barter, because Swedish traders could waylay the Minquas enroute to do business with the Dutch at Fort Nassau.

The Dutch retaliated by sending small barks or yachts across the river with the expectation of making contact with the Minquas parties ahead of the Swedes, but that was not a satisfactory solution. Hudde recommended that a more effective measure would be to settle colonists on the Schuylkill to secure the territory for the Dutch. Kieft, who concurred with Hudde's recommendation, immediately took steps to encourage Dutch freemen to move from New Amsterdam to the southern perimeter of what is now Greater Philadelphia and build houses and lay out farms.

To attract settlers Kieft offered them land free of charge provided they agreed to cultivate it within a year. He was also able to offer a second inducement; in May of 1639 the Amsterdam Chamber of the West India Company decided to allow private persons to barter with the Indians, superseding a former ruling that only the company could engage in the fur trade. That ruling gave Dutch settlers, both freemen and independent entrepreneurs, a distinct advantage over the Swedish settlers, because Printz rigidly enforced the New Sweden Company's policy of restricting the fur trade to the company. The colonists later accused him of violating his own rules.

The first four residents of New Amsterdam who took advantage of Kieft's offer were Abraham Planck, Symon Root, Jan Andriesen, and Peter Harmensen. They were granted 100 morgens of land, about 200 acres, for four boweries of fifty acres each. Thereafter, a number of others, including Hans Jacobsen, Thomas Broen, Cornelis Mauritsen, Philip Jansen, Peter Cornelissen, Reynier Dominicus, Sander Leendertsen, and Gerrit Hendricksen were given permission to lay out tracts and build houses. Some brought their wives and children with them. Peter Cornelissen and Reynier Dominicus were house carpenters who were able to build their own dwellings and assist those less skilled in carpentry. The names are all spelled here as they were given in the contemporary Dutch account, although they are spelled differently in other documents due to scribal inconsistencies.

It made no difference to Governor Printz that the intruders were private citizens not in the employ of the West India Company; they were, nevertheless, trespassers in territory claimed by Sweden. Printz also considered their activity a personal

affront because they erected their dwellings not far distant from his gubernatorial manse on Tinicum Island. He registered a strong protest to Hudde, who replied by letter stating that the territory belonged to the Dutch since they had occupied it long before the South River was heard of in Sweden. This was an exaggeration because there is no record of Dutch occupation of the Schuylkill watershed prior to the arrival of the Swedes on the Delaware, although the Dutch maintained that a former commander at Fort Nassau named Arent Corssen purchased land on the Schuylkill from the Lenape in 1633. No evidence of such purchase was produced, but there is no doubt that early Dutch explorers like Cornelis Hendricksen sailed in and out of the Schuylkill before New Sweden was founded.

Hudde, who had been invited as a dinner guest with his wife to Printzhoff following their arrival at Fort Nassau, signed his letter "your honor's affectionate friend." In view of the changes in Dutch policy, the friendly social relations between Printz and Hudde was probably of short duration!

The new director-general, Peter Stuyvesant, followed Kieft's example by encouraging Dutch freemen to build houses in the Schuylkill watershed. That made Printz furious and contributed to bad feelings between him and Stuyvesant. The situation grew progressively worse and reached a breaking point when Stuyvesant approved Hudde's recommendation that he be permitted to build a fortified trading post. Stuyvesant sent emissaries from New Amsterdam to buy the land from the Indians (even though Arent Corssen had allegedly bought it fifteen years before) so that he could confront Printz with Indian deeds to refute the Swedish governor's inevitable protests. Stuyvesant's representatives paid the Lenape chiefs with trade goods, and the Indians in turn made their marks on the parchment deeds formally written in Dutch legal language.

Hudde then erected the new fort on the east bank of the Schuylkill in the district known to the Lenape as Passyunk ("in the valley"), and named it Fort Beversreede, which means "beaver road" in Dutch. The name was derived from the path used by the Minquas to transport their furs, and the fort consisted of a trading house surrounded by log palisades. It was primarily intended as a commercial center where the Minquas could meet those Dutch who had goods to trade; the palisades were meant to protect the traders, as well as the pelts and trade goods, from hijackers.

The construction of Fort Beversreede on territory he was sworn to protect for his queen was an insult to Printz, but he was handicapped by limited manpower. He wrote in 1647 (the year Stuyvesant arrived in New Netherland) that the total population of New Sweden was only "183 souls," by which he meant men, women, and children. There had been deaths due to illness, Indian murders, and desertion—some of the families ran away from the colony to settle in Maryland. In letters to his superiors in Sweden he twice specifically urged that at least 100 soldiers be sent to strengthen his command, but no action was taken on his request. At one point he wrote that he had only thirty reliable men he could trust, and yet he was obliged to protect all of New Sweden, which at the time his Instruction was written in 1642, extended from Cape Henlopen on the west side of the Delaware River north to the Sankikans near Trenton, and on the east side from Narraticon Creek (present-day Raccoon Creek) south to Cape May. In 1649, Printz blocked expansion by Dutch freemen by buying land from the Indians between Narraticon Creek and Mantes Creek, which extended the bounds of New Sweden almost as far north as Fort Nassau.

The only practical way of meeting the Dutch threat was by deploying his men in surprise raids, since they had the advantage of a familiarity with the woods and creeks and the determination to thwart any intruders. One of the Swedes tore down the West India Company's coat of arms that Hudde had erected on lands purchased from the Indians, an unfriendly act then deemed a serious affront. Others pulled apart the houses under construction, destroyed timbers cut to build new houses, burnt down fences and newly planted fruit trees, uprooted gardens, seized boats, and confiscated powder and guns from Dutch traders.

Peter Jochim (Jochimsson), a soldier who lived at a place

called Aronameck on the west bank of the Schuylkill, tore down some of the palisades at Fort Beversreede after nightfall. When the Dutch replaced the palisades, the Swedes tore them down again and chopped up the wood. The Dutch again repaired the structure, and the Swedes retaliated by building a log block-house between the gate of Fort Beversreede and the river bank, which prevented ready access to the fort by both Dutch and Indians. Hudde's garrison at Fort Nassau was not strong enough to launch an attack against the Swedes, and he may have overestimated the number of defenders. Printz's officers were active participants in harassing the Dutch; the presence of Lieu-tenant Gustav Printz, the governor's son, Lieutenant Johan Papegoja, Lieutenant Måns Kling, Sergeant Gregorius van Dyck, and Commissary Hendrick Huygen probably gave the impression that Printz had more troops at his disposal than he really had. Actually those Swedish officers had to leave their permanent command posts at the major forts in order to handle the emergency. An enemy force might have easily captured Fort Elfsborg, Fort Christina, Fort New Gothenburg, and Nya Korsholm with their commanders absent, but this was a risk Printz had to take.

Although Stuyvesant had taken an aggressive stand, he no doubt cautioned Hudde to avoid bloodshed or initiating overt action construed to antagonize the Swedish Crown. Like Kieft, he did not want to be responsible for an act of war that would disrupt the friendly relations then existing between Sweden and Holland. He did not have to be reminded of Sweden's retalia-tory power as the leading military nation in northern Europe. However, it didn't take very long for Stuyvesant to conclude from the reports he received that Printz was not being supported from Sweden with the supplies and soldiers he needed and that his forces were inadequate to repel a major attack. Nevertheless, Printz's forts were so expertly positioned that Fort Elfsborg outflanked Fort Nassau; Fort Christina controlled access to the Minquas Kill; and the Swedish fortified posts on the tributaries of the Schuylkill dominated that important Minquas trade route.

SALEM RIVER
(New Jersey)

(Delaware)

ANDERS DITCH

LOCATION OF FORT ELFSBORG
? ? ? ?

MILL CREEK

NO ONE BUT THE DELAWARE RIVER REALLY KNOWS!

WICACO BLOCKHOUSE

THE BLOCK HOUSE

SKETCHED FROM A WOODCUT IN 2ND EDITION OF REV. JEHU CURTIS' *ANNALS OF THE SWEDES ON THE DELAWARE* (1858)

POSSIBLE DESIGN OF
FORT ELFSBORG

OCT. 13, 1643 "sailed by Reed Island, and came to Vercken's Kill where there was a fort constructed by the Swedes with three angles from which they fired on us to strike our flag."
—DAVID PETER DEVRIES

FORT CASIMIR →

BUILT ON THE SITE OF PRESENT DAY NEW CASTLE BY THE DUTCH IN 1651. IT FELL TO THE SWEDES IN 1654. IT WAS RE-CLAIMED BY THE DUTCH IN 1655.

GUNPORTS WERE NARROW SLOTS OR LOOPHOLES. IT IS BELIEVED THE DEFENDERS FIRED FROM AN INSIDE PLATFORM REACHED BY STEPS CUT FROM A SOLID LOG.

GOVERNOR PRINTZ IN A REPORT OF JUNE 11, 1644 CALLED IT "a strong wooden house with small stone cannon".

[A "STONE CANNON" FIRED ROUND STONES INSTEAD OF METAL BALLS]

THE BLOCKHOUSE AT UPLAND

SAWIN

Placing Dutch settlers in enemy country, as Hudde recommended, was not a practical solution to the Swedish problen.

Poring over his maps and charts in New Amsterdam, Stuyvesant laid his own plans for more effective action. After secret but thorough preparation, he marched overland to Fort Nassau with a force of 120 soldiers. No army of such size had ever before been seen on the Delaware River. It may not sound like a formidable number, but the ratio of the force to the total population of the New Netherland was about 10 percent, which proportionately measured against the total male population of the United States today, was an unprecedented military manpower never since equaled.

At Fort Nassau, Stuyvesant and his army had a prearranged rendezvous with eleven Dutch vessels that had sailed down the coast from the harbor at New Amsterdam, into Delaware Bay, and up the river to join him.

In *Swedes and Dutch at New Castle*, this author referred to these vessels as follows:

This first flotilla of "tall ships" in the Delaware must have been spectacular, one riding in the wake of another, sails bellied in the wind with the flags of the Prince of Orange and the West India Company streaming from their masts. The vessels encountered no resistance as they followed a single-file course up the river from Cape Henlopen. Not a single cannon was fired fron Fort Elfsborg. Lieutenant Sven Skute had been sent back to Sweden by Printz to make a report to the colony. The garrison he left at Elfsborg consisted of five or six frightened Swedes who apparently did not dare fire on what appeared to be an unconquerable fleet sent by one of the world's greatest maritime powers.

After reaching Fort Nassau the ships, on Stuyvesant's orders, sailed part way down the river again, firing their cannon to the noise of beating drums. Printz scarcely had time to summon Lieutenants Papegoja, Kling, and Gustav Printz to a strategy meeting at Printzhoff, but there was little to be done. The invasion forces capable of attacking by both land and water not only greatly outnumbered Printz's military forces, but the num-

ber of Dutch soldiers and seamen was actually two or three
times larger than the total population of New Sweden. Discretion being the better part of valor, Printz offered no resistance.

That was what Stuyvesant anticipated would be the response
to his threatened attack. He never really intended to fight; in
fact, only four of the vessels were well-armed for battle duty.
Printz did not know that until later, but it would not have made
any difference. By sheer bravado and a display of military
strength Stuyvesant, in effect, conquered New Sweden without
shedding a drop of blood. He outwitted the Swedish warrior
who had enlisted as a sergeant in the Swedish army many years
before and who after a long military career had been promoted
to the rank of a lieutenant-colonel for his bravery.

Stuyvesant did not order his troops to take any of the Swedish
forts nor to do any damage to the houses and farms of the
Swedish settlers. He did not molest Printz nor any of his
soldiers or officers. All Stuyvesant had done was to conduct a
maneuver—a peaceful war game that harmed no one but established his mastery. Yet he had another objective, which soon
became apparent to Governor Printz.

About six miles south of Fort Christina, on the west bank of
the Delaware River, there was an unusual topographical feature
known to both Dutch and Swedes as the Santhoeck. The word
means "sand point," not "sand hook," and it was used to
describe a tapered earthen promontory covered with a sandy
mantle that extended out into the river. The front bank facing
the river arose vertically from a narrow beach, where the water
was deep enough for sailing vessels to anchor and unload their
cargoes without the need of smaller landing craft. Nothing
remains of that point today—it has long since been eroded away
by the weather and tides—but we know it was located beyond the
end of present-day Chestnut Street in New Castle.

Stuyvesant decided to build a major Dutch fort at the Santhoeck
and also to establish a Dutch town there. A fort at that site would
have military advantages that Fort Nassau lacked; its cannon
would render useless the cannon at Fort Elfsborg on the opposite side of the river; it could sever the lines of communication

between Fort Elfsborg and Fort New Gothenburg on Tinicum Island; and it could isolate the garrison at Fort Christina from the Delaware. The site had the economic advantage of a deep harbor where both coastal and ocean-going vessels could anchor, and it was on the west side of the river, which was more convenient for the Minquas traders than Fort Nassau on the opposite bank. The fort would also be a citadel to protect the Dutch town Stuyvesant visualized. His decision to build a fort at the Santhoeck was a brilliant military stroke designed to checkmate Printz and his unwelcome Swedes. Printz's mistake was that he did not recognize the strategic value of the Santhoeck eight years earlier when he erected forts intended to control the river.

Stuyvesant did not have Indian deeds for the Santhoeck, an area then known to the Lenape by two names, Tamakonck ("place of the beaver") and Quinamkot ("a sandy area that is long"). It did not take him long to correct that omission. He rounded up the Lenape chiefs and bought all the land from the Minquas Kill along the west shore of the Delaware as far south as Bombay Hook for "twelve coats of duffels, twelve kettles, twelve axes, 12 adzes, 24 knives, 12 bars of lead [for making bullets], and four guns and some powder." Stuyvesant agreed that the Indians could retain their hunting and fishing rights to the area, which they now insisted on as a concession to protect their livelihood. The Indians signed the deed with their marks in a ceremony at the Santhoeck that was witnessed by a number of Dutch leaders who accompanied Stuyvesant on the expedition. It did not seem to matter to anyone except Governor Printz (who was not present) that the Swedes had deeds to the identical land in the chancery at Stockholm. There was not much Printz could do except to protest, and those protests did not deter Stuyvesant. Hudde had already surveyed the site, and before the ink on the parchment was dry, 200 soldiers, sailors, carpenters, and laborers were already at work.

The deed with the Indians was signed July 19, 1651, and the size of the working force permitted the practical completion of the fort before the end of the month. Fort Nassau was dismantled; its cannon, usable timbers, trade goods, officers, soldiers, and freemen, with their families and possessions, were moved down the river to the new location. Fort Beversreede was also vacated. Among the Dutch formerly settled on the Schuylkill the names of Peter Harmensen, Symon Root, Thomas Broen, Reynier Dominicus, Cornelis Mauritsen, and Sander (Alexander) Boyer subsequently appear in the records as residents at the Santhoeck. Sander Boyer, incidentally, was conversant in the Lenape dialect and acted as Stuyvesant's interpreter in his conferences with the Indians.

Stuyvesant named the new fortress Fort Casimir, although no records explain why he chose that name. Count Ernst Casimir, Earl of Nassau-Dietz, and a distinguished stadholder in Friesland, Stuyvesant's home province, was a military hero during Stuyvesant's boyhood; the fort was doubtless named in his memory. If any drawings were made of Fort Casimir none has survived. Speculations have been made about its size and shape, but it is all conjectural. There is no doubt that it was palisaded and that a storehouse, barracks for the soldiers, and several dwellings were built within the palisades. It was a sizeable and well-armed citadel; after it was finished Printz wrote that the Dutch were able to detain and collect a toll from all foreign vessels, because, as he phrased it, Stuyvesant ''masters the whole river.'' That, in effect, meant that New Sweden was landlocked if Stuyvesant so willed it.

Before he sailed back to New Amsterdam with his flotilla, Stuyvesant named Sergeant Gerrit Bicker the commandant at Fort Casimir and placed Andries Hudde in charge of civilian affairs. The number of Dutch soldiers left at the fort is not known, but the garrison was large enough, and there was sufficient armament, to prevent the Swedes from attempting any mischief. But just to make sure, Stuyvesant temporarily left two armed vessels at the fort.

After Printz's arrival in 1644 as governor of the colony, vessels from Sweden brought supplies, a few new settlers, and letters from his superiors. The *Swan*, which the reader will recall arrived at Fort Christina in 1648, was the last vessel to bring him supplies from the homeland. After that he received no reinforcements, no goods for the Indian trade, and no letters.

In the summer of 1649 plans were made in Sweden to send supplies and reinforcements to Printz; consideration was given to preparing the *Kalmar Nyckel* for her fourth voyage to the Delaware. The venerable vessel had seen Swedish service for more than seventeen years, and it was decided she was too old and unseaworthy for another Atlantic crossing. The ship selected for the mission was another one owned by the government, *Kattan* (*The Cat*), and she sailed from Gothenburg on July 31. With a crew of about fifty sailors, she carried seventy passengers, including women and children, and a cargo of provisions, cloth, shoes, tools, and other supplies Printz needed.

When she reached the Caribbean, the *Cat* stopped at Antigua, Saint Kitts, and Saint Martin without mishap, but in waters near Puerto Rico she ran aground on a sunken reef. Spaniards confiscated all the cargo that could be salvaged, set the ship afire, and carried off passengers and crew. The Swedes were badly treated in Puerto Rico; about forty-five or fifty were killed or died from abuse or lack of medical care. Eventually about nineteen persons made their way back to Sweden. One of the survivors was the barber-surgeon Timen Stiddem. It was a disastrous voyage for Stiddem because his wife and three small children died in Puerto Rico, according to a letter he wrote Chancellor Oxenstierna from Gothenburg on his return.

The ill-fated voyage of the *Cat* was disastrous for colony and company. No supplies or reinforcements reached Printz, and the voyage was a costly loss to the government and the company. Deprived of support from the homeland, Printz had to fall back on his own ingenuity and the resourcefulness of his followers to sustain the colony. He was able to bargain with friendly English merchants for food and supplies, including sewant to use in the Indian trade. The lack of trade goods from Sweden depressed commerce with the Minquas and tended to alienate the Lenape, who were denied the periodic presents they had learned to expect from the Swedes.

Why did the Swedish government not send other ships and reinforcements when they learned of the calamity that had befallen the *Cat?* What had happened in Sweden to cause the indifference to Printz's numerous letters asking for support? Why was the colony being allowed to dry on the vine?

First of all, Queen Christina took little interest in the colony. She was more concerned with making the Swedish court famous for its balls, masques, and pageants than in supporting New Sweden in the American wilderness. She nearly bankrupted the kingdom with her reckless spending of royal revenues. The war with Denmark diverted ships, supplies, and money for military purposes; the death of Admiral Fleming deprived the colony of its greatest champion. The New Sweden Company lacked leadership and initiative; no one seemed to understand that Printz was unable to maintain the colony unaided.

Printz was left to his own devices to rule a dying colony beleagured by a stronger rival. He did his best to make New Sweden self-supporting agriculturally. Grain and Indian corn had become more important to the colonists than tobacco-raising, but there were periods of too much rain, as well as times of droughts, when there was inadequate food for the soldiers, company employees, and freemen. Only Printz's bargaining with the English for edibles prevented starvation.

As the chief executive and legislative officer, as well as the prosecuting attorney and judge, Printz ruled as an autocrat, making all the decisions affecting the colony. It is true that in a report sent to Sweden in 1647 he requested that a learned and able man be sent to handle the judicial business in the colony because it was not proper for him to prosecute a case and then sit in judgement of the accused, but no one was sent to assist him. His request for assistance, however, does not excuse him from the despotic action that caused some of the Swedes and Finns to flee from the colony and settle in Maryland. Nor does it provide justification for the grievances that were enumerated in a supplication of eleven articles signed by twenty-two colonists and presented to him on July 27, 1653.

The colonists accused Printz of brutality and avarice; of

forbidding them from grinding their flour at the mill; of making legal decisions in his own favor; of prohibiting them access to the trees in the woods, the grass on the ground, the land to plant on, and the waters in which to fish. They complained he would not permit them to trade with the Indians whereas he personally sold large quantities of beaver skins to the English for gold and also sent pelts to Holland to be credited to his personal account.

The petition aroused Printz's anger, and he arrested Anders Jönsson, who seems to have been the leader of the opposition, and executed him for treason. That action calmed down what might have become a mutiny, but the resentment toward Printz was not lessened. Possibly some of the complaints were exaggerated, perhaps unfounded, but there must have been a basic cause for the colonists' displeasure with their governor. Printz had the power to invoke the death penalty but, according to his Instruction, only "after a careful hearing and consideration of the case with the foremost people and the most prudent associate judges who can be found in the country for assistance and counsel." Evidence is lacking that Anders Jönsson was given a fair trial before the death sentence was pronounced.

Printz had repeatedly requested that he be relieved of his command on the Delaware, reminding his superiors that after three years he was free to return "after the necessary arrangement had been made for his successor." While he was still in direct contact with the homeland he was told to remain at his post for a few more years because no worthy successor could be found. The three years turned into nine, and during the last six years he did not receive a single letter or message from Sweden!

In the beginning of October 1653 he decided to initiate action himself. He gathered together his personal belongings and went with his wife and four of his daughters to New Amsterdam, where he arranged for transatlantic passage on a Dutch vessel. He was accompanied by about twenty-five soldiers and settlers, including his chief commissary, Hendrick Huygen, who was a member of Minuit's original expedition in 1638. Printz left New Sweden in charge of his son-in-law, Lieutenant Papegoja, whose wife, Armegot, remained with him. Printz promised he would return within ten or twelve months, or at least arrange for a ship to be sent from Sweden to bring relief to the colony. The total population remaining in New Sweden consisted of less than a hundred men, women, and children—not enough to cause Stuyvesant any worry. Indeed, Stuyvesant had his hands full with the New Englanders and was preoccupied with strengthening his command at New Amsterdam against a possible English attack. In fact, he was forced to withdraw some of the soldiers from Fort Casimir. Although Santhoeck remained under Dutch control, Stuyvesant was unable to enlarge the settlement there as he had originally planned.

7. RISING CAPTURES FORT CASIMIR

Governor Printz did not know it, but interest in the Delaware colony had been revived in Sweden, and while he was in the midst of making plans to return home, a new expedition was being organized to bring settlers, food, and supplies for his relief. A branch of the government known as the Commercial College, which functioned as a national Board of Trade, was given the management of the New Sweden Company. A special function of the Commercial College was to promote foreign trade. Eric Oxenstierna, son of the chancellor, was named general director in 1652 and became a leading force in the movement to rejuvenate the colony. Eric Oxenstierna recommended that Johan Rising, the secretary of the Commercial College, be placed in charge of the expedition. Rising (pronounced Ree-sing), an economist and a recognized authority on commerce, trade, and agriculture, had studied commercial systems in a number of European countries he had visited. That background made him the ideal candidate. He accepted the offer to serve with Printz in New Sweden as commissary and assistant councillor, an office that might be compared to a lieutenant-governor. Before Rising left Sweden, Queen Christina knighted him, giving him the status of a nobleman, and invested him with a personal tract of land on the Delaware.

Lieutenant Sven Skute, who was still in Sweden after delivering Printz's report on the progress, or lack of it, in the colony, was assigned to hire soldiers and workmen and to assist in enrolling farmers to accompany Rising to New Sweden. The government inaugurated a new policy of excluding criminals and lawbreakers from the expedition, which was in sharp contrast to the earlier expeditions. That change in national policy could reflect a different attitude on the part of some respectable Swedes about leaving their homes and going to America. A decline in the Swedish economy and the famines of 1650–51, with a shortage of grains, may have been factors that caused heads of families to seek the new opportunities offered in America. There may have been other reasons not now fully understood. For instance, a plague caused illness and death in the eastern part of Sweden, and even Queen Christina left Stockholm and went to Uppsala to escape the epidemic, and that might have been another factor. Whatever the reasons, there was no difficulty in enrolling colonists for the expedition. More than a hundred families, who had sold their belongings in anticipation of migrating, were turned away at the last moment because a change of plans delayed the sailing of one of the vessels.

The Commercial College planned to send two vessels, the Örn (*Eagle*), owned by the Admiralty, and the *Gyllene Haj* (*Golden Shark*), a galleon owned by the New Sweden Company, or the "new" South Company, as it was now called in a revival of the old name. The *Örn*, the larger of the two vessels, was a thirty-four to forty cannon warship that had been taken in the war with the Danes and completely rerigged. As the time neared for departure, the *Haj* was not yet in sea-faring condition. Some of her intended passengers were transferred to the *Örn*, which sailed from Gothenburg alone on February 2, 1654, overcrowded with 350 people. Her cargo consisted of goods for use in the Indian trade, clothing, muskets, implements, and tools for the colonists. She carried wine and beer, the staple beverages of the day, for consumption en route, as well as a limited quantity of bread, butter, and other foodstuffs. Space that would normally have been used for transporting food was alloted for passengers, because the revised schedule called for the *Haj* to follow as soon as possible with a cargo of food.

Before the *Örn* departed, news reached Sweden that Governor Printz was on his way back home but had fallen ill in Holland. After leaving New Amsterdam, Printz and his party were at sea for more than ten weeks due to unfavorable winds. Adverse winter weather finally forced the captain to make a landing in France. After six weeks in France, Printz sailed to Amsterdam, where he remained for several additional weeks, finally arriving in Gothenburg on April 24, long after the *Örn* had sailed. Stuyvesant in far-off America received a letter from the directors of the West India Company dated May 18, 1654, advising him that they assessed Printz an import duty for the large quantity of beaver pelts that he sold in Amsterdam, the profits of which he invested in his personal account. That might seem to support the charge made by the twenty-two irate colonists that he engaged in private fur trading, but whether he did so to the detriment of the Swedish government is questionable. There is the possibility he may have considered the pelts reimbursement for business expenses that he personally incurred in the colony.

If Printz was guilty of malfeasance, no charges were ever brought against him in Stockholm, nor was he rebuked for leaving his American command without specific orders. Quite the contrary, the members of the Council of State must have sympathized with the hardships he endured, for he was promoted to a full colonel and then in 1658 was appointed governor of the Jönköping district, one of the highest offices to which he could aspire—a position he held until his death in 1663.

Rising, of course, had no opportunity to discuss the political situation in New Sweden with his predecessor. It was known from Printz's letters that Stuyvesant had invaded the colony and built Fort Casimir, but Rising had no way of knowing whether Stuyvesant subsequently seized Fort Christina, Fort Elfsborg, or Fort New Gothenburg. That worriment must have weighed heavily on him from the day the *Örn* broke through the ice in the Gothenburg harbor and headed out to sea.

The *Örn's* maiden voyage to America was a tragic one. An epidemic broke out on the ship, possibly the same contagion experienced in eastern Sweden, and in early March some of the passengers showed signs of illness. Before the ship reached the Delaware Bay, more than a hundred persons had died and been buried at sea. Peter Lindeström, a twenty-one-year-old engineer who had studied mathematics and the science of fortifications at Uppsala University, kept a journal in which he recorded the terrible storms and the harrowing experiences suffered by passengers and crew during the three-month voyage. "We thought that death would be the fate of us all," he wrote.

On March 20, 1654, the *Örn* made a landing in the Canary Islands, where fresh water, oranges, lemons, bananas, yams, and other foods were taken aboard. There Rising learned from the Spanish governor that he had been informed through diplomatic channels that Queen Christina intended to give up her throne and go to Rome to live as a Roman Catholic. If Gustavus Adolphus, the champion of Protestantism, were alive, he would not have taken kindly to his daughter's conversion, but Christina had her own reasons and a will of her own.

On May 20, the *Örn* anchored in the Delaware River opposite Fort Elfsborg, which Rising found deserted and in ruins. That destruction could not be blamed on the Dutch, who never attacked the citadel. If we can believe Lindeström, hordes of mosquitos that bred in the marshes of New Jersey made life so miserable for the members of the Swedish garrison that they fell sick and could get no rest or sleep during the day or night. The situation became so unbearable that they were forced to vacate the post that Printz had built as the keystone of his defenses. They gave the hollow shell a new name—"Mosquito Fort."

When Sergent Gerrit Bicker, the commandant at Fort Casimir, saw the *Örn* in the river he dispatched five Dutchmen in a small boat to investigate from whence she came and the purpose of her mission. Rising welcomed them aboard the *Örn* and learned that Fort Christina and Fort New Gothenburg were still in Swedish hands but that the Dutch controlled Fort Casimir, which was in disrepair. Stuyvesant had given priority to strengthening his defenses at New Amsterdam due to the threat of an English attack, so the garrison at Fort Casimir had been reduced to nine Dutch soldiers, and there was no powder for the thirteen cannon intended to defend the river! In that weakness, Rising recognized his opportunity to assert Swedish rights without the risk of provoking war, which he had been instructed to avoid.

Neither the Commercial College nor the Council of State approved of Rising initiating aggressive action that might cause a rupture between New Sweden and the Netherlands. That position had been communicated to him in writing, although there was a certain vagueness in how he could secure both sides of the river, as stated in the orders, "without hostility." If the Dutch could not be removed "by argument and grave remonstrances," whatever that meant, he was told it would be better to avoid a confrontation and erect another Swedish stronghold south of the Dutch fort. To have followed those instructions would have been an expensive folly. Stuyvesant would never have allowed a Swedish fort to block Dutch access to the Delaware; it would eventually have been taken, as proved by subsequent events.

Rising was not a man to act rashly, and he fully understood that his government strongly opposed Dutch control of New Sweden. If the situation so indicated he was authorized to take possession of Fort Casimir by "arguing" for the Swedish right to it without using violence. He consulted with the three principal leaders on his staff: Sven Skute, promoted to a captain before leaving Sweden and given the title "Commander of the Military"; Lieutenant Elias Gyllengren, son-in-law of Hans Amundsson, a prominent ship captain; and Peter Lindeström, who then had no official rank but was later commissioned engineer and clerk of the court. They agreed with Rising on a subject he had discussed with Eric Oxenstierna and others; namely, the English must not be allowed to dominate the Delaware valley. The weakness of the garrison at Fort Casimir and its inadequate armament made the territory vulnerable to seizure by the English if they took New Amsterdam. Rising's officers supported his plan of persuading Bicker to "deliver" the fort to them on the basis that "it had been built on Swedish territory by Stuyvesant on his own initiative without orders from his superiors."

Rising accurately characterized the situation, because in his bloodless invasion of 1651 Stuyvesant had leveled Fort Nassau and built Fort Casimir without the knowledge of the directors of the West India Company. When the directors learned what Stuyvesant had done, they were astonished at the apparent imprudent act and wrote him stating that they hoped things would turn out for the best. They were thinking of what the reaction would be in Stockholm to what the Swedes might consider an overtly unfriendly act.

The next morning, Trinity Sunday, May 21, following religious services aboard ship, the *Örn* crossed the river and saluted the Dutch fort by firing two of her cannon. There was no answer from the fort, which was probably a relief to the tired and ailing passengers who must have feared suffering casualties in a gun battle before reaching their destination. Captain Skute and Lieutenant Gyllengren went ashore with twenty or thirty musketeers. Bicker met them without offering any resistance, and Skute, as he had been coached by Rising, entered into a lengthy discussion with the Dutch commander. Messages went back and forth from the fort to Rising, who remained aboard the *Örn*. The result was that Bicker "delivered" the fort to the Swedes without bloodshed. The Swedish colors were run up the mast to replace the Dutch flag, and Rising named the citadel Fort Trefaldighet ("Fort Trinity") because of the religious holiday. Rising later maintained the transition was made without hostility and that the Dutch garrison and the settlers were guaranteed freedom for their persons, property, occupations, and religion. They were all given the option of leaving unharmed if they elected to do so.

Bicker, who was later charged with disloyalty, testified in his own defense that he was forced to capitulate because he had no powder and was outnumbered by the Swedish forces, who took the muskets and sidearms away from his men, forcibly seized the cannon, and threatened to turn the *Örn's* cannon on the fort. Rising denied this, but whether he did or did not commit a hostile act is a matter of definition; the act of taking the fort was no more or less hostile than Stuyvesant's act in building it.

Neither operation involved hand-to-hand encounters or any casualties. The important result was that the Swedes were once more in possession of the Delaware valley, and Rising had achieved it without a clash of arms.

At that time there were twenty-one or twenty-two houses outside the fort occupied by Dutch civilians, but the Swedish soldiers did no injury to them or their properties. Rising left Lieutenant Gyllengren, supported by the Swedish musketeers, in command of the fort, and he sailed up to Fort Christina where he conferred with Vice-Director Johan Papegoja. The passengers on the *Örn* were taken ashore; some were quartered in the buildings at Fort Christina and others were taken in by Swedish and Finnish families living on farms along the creek shores. Some of those hospitable folk fell victims to the contagion brought by the newcomers. The epidemic also spread to the Lenape families, leading the chiefs to blame the Swedes for bringing an evil Manito on their ship to destroy the Indians.

Rising learned from Papegoja that Printz's severity, and the scarcity of food and consumer goods, had a depressing effect on the morale in the colony. At least fifteen colonists, some with families, deserted and settled in Maryland after Printz's departure. Taking into consideration those who returned to Sweden with Printz, there were only about seventy persons remaining in the colony when Rising arrived. The soldiers, servants, and freemen who debarked from the *Örn* with Rising suddenly escalated the population to more than 300 men, women, and children, but many were too ill to work.

Rising set up a provisional government consisting of himself (the Swedish government later named him "Director of New Sweden"), Captain Skute, and Vice-Director Johan Papegoja. The latter's military rank as a lieutenant subordinated him to Skute, who was second in command, but Rising's orders directed him to consult other "good men" as needed, and Papegoja's experience was an important asset no less valuable than Skute's.

On May 23—two days after Fort Casimir was delivered—Sergeant Bicker, Andries Hudde, the soldiers in the Dutch

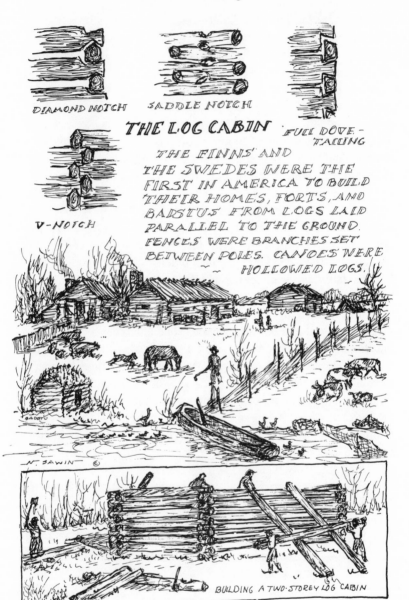

DIAMOND NOTCH

SADDLE NOTCH

THE LOG CABIN

FULL DOVE-TAILING

V-NOTCH

THE FINNS' AND THE SWEDES WERE THE FIRST IN AMERICA TO BUILD THEIR HOMES, FORTS, AND BARNS FROM LOGS LAID PARALLEL TO THE GROUND. FENCES WERE BRANCHES SET BETWEEN POLES. CANOES WERE HOLLOWED LOGS.

N. SAWIN ©

BUILDING A TWO-STOREY LOG CABIN

garrison, and the colonists residing in the houses at the Santhoeck came to Fort Christina and took an oath that they would be loyal and true Swedish subjects thereafter. Rising wrote that he welcomed them as honest neighbors and citizens. The Dutch were under no compulsion to take the oath; in fact, six of the soldiers said they preferred to return to New Amsterdam, and Rising gave them permission to do so. Hudde agreed to assist Rising by making maps and drawings of the river for a fee of twenty Florins, and with a few exceptions relations between Dutch and Swedes seemed to be harmonious, at least on the surface. After the Dutch colonists returned to the Santhoeck they became restless in time; nevertheless, they twice confirmed their oath of allegiance when Rising confronted them with reports that he had heard they claimed he coerced them into signing the document.

Skute, assisted by Lindeström, who had been taught the latest fortification techniques at Uppsala, took over a project to remodel and renovate Fort Trinity. New bastions were constructed and a rampart built on the river side in front of the fort proper, where four cannon taken from the *Örn* were positioned. During the construction work all the male residents were required to contribute fourteen work days to the project. That probably caused some resentment and contributed to Dutch unhappiness. Rising also held a court in a room at Fort Trinity (he also held court at Fort Christina and on Tinicum Island), and the Dutch may not have relished having their legal matters adjudicated by a tribunal headed by foreigners. There was also the likelihood that cooperation with the Swedish trespassers would displease Stuyvesant, who might consider their actions treasonable. It was no secret that Stuyvesant was infuriated when he learned that Rising had occupied the fort.

One after another the Dutch settlers left the Santhoeck to go to New Amsterdam, taking advantage of the option Rising yielded to them. In a report dated June 14, 1655, Rising said that two or three weeks prior to that date the last of the Dutch families vacated their homes, because they "were out of their element here in the river." The houses they abandoned at Fort Trinity were taken over by Swedish and Finnish families. A number of the Scandinavians also settled on the Niew Claerlandh ("Newly Cleared Land") along the river between present Crane Hook and Fort Trinity near a place called Strand Wyck, which was near present-day Swanwyck. The Swedish pastor, the Reverend Peter Hiört, who had arrived with Rising on the *Örn,* was assigned to Fort Trinity to conduct Lutheran services for the Swedes and Finns in the environs. At the time there was no Dutch Reformed pastor at the Santhoeck, and the Dutch residents must have felt like outsiders in the renaissance of New Sweden. It is not difficult to understand why they left the Delaware to rejoin their own countrymen on Manhattan Island.

Johan Printz conducted a semi-military governorship of New Sweden, always mindful of the tactical advantage of well-placed forts and the importance of maintaining a strong command. He never relented in his recommendations for more soldiers, although his requests did not materialize. Rising was not a military man, and as an economist his emphasis was in positioning the colony for increased commerce. After his arrival, he made an announcement of a policy change agreed upon by the government before he left Sweden—an announcement enthusiastically received by the colonists. Private colonists would thereafter be permitted to trade with the Indians or other Europeans, and they were also given the right to buy land from the company, or the Indian owners if the land had not already been conveyed to the company. There had never been serious differences about land tenure in New Sweden because land was plentiful and a farmer improved and cultivated the land of his choice and built a house on it. The new regulation was intended to guarantee the rights of an individual by officially transferring perpetual ownership to the purchaser and his heirs. Rising lacked the authority to issue patents for land to the settlers, although he recognized the ownership interest in the improvements that a resident made on the land such as the erection of houses, fences, planting fruit trees, etc. The next step would have been to formalize title deeds in fee simple, but New Sweden fell before the government delegated that authority to him.

Opening up the fur trade gave the colonists the opportunity to

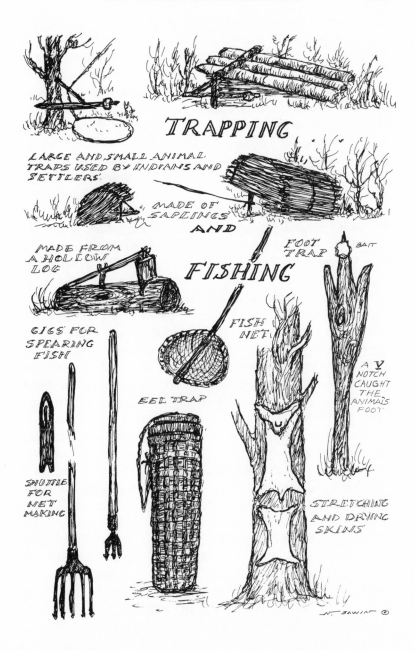

TRAPPING

LARGE AND SMALL ANIMAL TRAPS USED BY INDIANS AND SETTLERS

MADE OF SAPLINGS

MADE FROM A HOLLOW LOG

FOOT TRAP

BAIT

AND

FISHING

GIGS FOR SPEARING FISH

FISH NET

A V NOTCH CAUGHT THE ANIMAL'S FOOT

EEL TRAP

SHUTTLE FOR NET MAKING

STRETCHING AND DRYING SKINS

N. SAWIN ©

barter not only with the Lenape and Minquas, but also with other tribes, such as the Mohawks, from whom Dutch traders at Fort Orange (present Albany) had been obtaining thousands of beaver pelts each year. The Dutch lost much of that business because of the preoccupation in New Amsterdam with an anticipated English attack. Of course Rising wanted to develop as much of the fur business as possible on behalf of the Commercial College, but he also recognized the need for economic diversification in New Sweden. In his first report, which Johan Papegoja took back home with him to Sweden when the *Örn* left the Delaware on July 15, 1654, Rising outlined some of those objectives.

Rising pointed out that the waterpower provided at the falls in the Brandywine Creek, which was known to the Swedes as the Fiskiekijlen ("the Fish River"), could be harnessed to operate a flour mill, a saw mill, a chamois-dressing mill, and an enterprise that had to await the ingenuity of a French immigrant named du Pont 150 years later—a powder mill. Rising wrote that if he could obtain sufficient saltpeter and could build a powder mill, it "would bring us a great profit." He also said that a brewery, a distillery, alehouses, and well-designed inns could provide a good profit. Moreover, if the abundant timber growing on all sides in the Delaware valley could be sawed in a mill into planks, clapboards, and barrel staves, a profitable trade could be developed with the Caribbean countries. He visualized the acceleration of ship commerce between Sweden and the colony, with vessels bringing both linens and cheaper fabrics in demand in America and returning with "tobacco, calmus, sassafras, sugar, figs, and other goods" to be sold in the Swedish market.

He stressed the opportunity for supplying other market needs with the products of pottery makers, brick makers, lime burners, cabinet makers, wooden-basin makers, shoemakers, and tanners. He pointed out that improved returns would result from increasing farming and cattle raising, and he said he was already at work clearing the land north of Fort Christina for a town projected by Lindeström, who made plans for dividing it into building lots. A map drawn by Lindeström at Rising's direction showing Fort Christina and the town plan was taken back to the Commercial College on the *Örn*, and it is still preserved in the Royal Archives in Sweden. Six or eight houses were later built as the nucleus of the projected town named Christinahamn ("Christina Harbor"), but the village never grew as planned. Rising also put the soldiers and laborers to work repairing Fort Christina by erecting new turf ramparts on two of the sides, replacing the old rotting palisades with new ones, and putting up a storehouse, built over a cellar dug in the fort, where provisions could be kept. Repairs were also made on some of the decayed log dwellings in the fort.

Rising did not agree with Printz's choice of Tinicum Island as the "capital" of New Sweden. Also, of course, the island was Printz's property, which precluded Rising from taking up land there. Rising decided to use the principal dwelling at Fort Christina as his temporary headquarters. Before Rising left Sweden, Queen Christina granted him a tract south of Crane Hook large enough to be cultivated by twenty or thirty peasants, but he found the site too remote from Fort Christina. He selected another tract closer to the fort lying between the north side of the Brandywine and Skillpaddekylen ("Mudturtle Creek," present-day Shellpot Creek) known as Timmer Island ("Timber Island"). Due to topographical changes it is difficult to imagine that there was once an island here, even one separated from the mainland by a narrow creek. Rising built a two-story manse on his island estate, probably of hewn logs because of the shortage of bricks and boards, and his servants planted corn, tobacco, and fruit trees. At that time, following her husband's return to Sweden, Armegot Printz Papegoja moved from Fort Christina to live at Printzhoff with her children.

The notion that Fort Christina was the center of the Swedish occupancy is incorrect, because the majority of the Swedes and Finns were settled at Chester, Marcus Hook, Essington, Kingsessing, and along Cobbs and Darby creeks. The former Dutch settlement at present-day New Castle continued to attract Scandinavian families, but the religious hub of New Sweden was still at the Lutheran church on Tinicum Island, where Pastor Matthias Nertunius conducted the services. It is true that during Rising's administration Pastor Lock held services at Fort Christina, but contemporary records make no reference to a church building there or at New Castle. The probability is that Lock may have officiated in the chapel at Fort Christina (or simply Christina, as it came to be known) built during Ridder's administration. It is not unlikely that Printz may have authorized renovating and decorating the chapel to make it appear more church-like since he was responsive to the spiritual needs of the people living in the vicinity.

The first true Swedish Lutheran church in what is now the state of Delaware was a log building erected south of the Christina River at Crane Hook in 1667. It accomodated members of a small community that sprang up there, but members of the congregation also included families living in the area from Naaman's Creek on the north as far south as Appoquinimink Creek. The Crane Hook Church was supplanted in 1699 by Holy Trinity (Old Swedes) Church, which was built after the fall of New Sweden.

Rising held a number of civic meetings at the church on Tinicum Island following the services conducted by the Reverend Nertunius, who, like Pastor Hiört, had come with Rising on the *Örn*. Rising moved back and forth from Fort Christina to Fort Trinity and Tinicum Island as need required, to hold courts and conduct other business. For instance, on June 9, 1654, a day set aside for feasting and prayer in the colony, he went up to Tinicum to attend church, and following the services he summoned all the freemen, male and female, young and old. He told them he was aware of the discontent that had occurred during the Printz admimistration, and he knew that some persons had run away and others had signed a petition complaining about Printz. He said that the facts were known in Sweden, where Printz could defend his actions and where the case would be resolved. He asked for their support and hoped that they would all remain faithful Swedish subjects and not desert the colony. At his request forty-eight of his listeners signed an oath swearing loyalty to Queen Christina, but little did the signatories know that the queen was then preparing for her abdication ceremony and would shortly be succeeded by her cousin Crown Prince Charles (subsequently Charles X).

Among those who signed the oath were eight widows, one whose husband, Mans Svensson Lom, came on the *Kalmar Nyckel* in 1641. The other seven possibly lost their husbands on the *Örn*, and six of the male signers were marked "sick," indicating the illness had not abated. The widow women did not have to worry about getting new husbands—men always outnumbered women in the colony and practically all widows remarried. Single girls also became wives at a young age, often sixteen or seventeen. Rising, who was a bachelor, apparently could not find a helpmate who pleased him, so he wrote Eric Oxenstierna to try to locate a suitable wife in Sweden willing to come to America.

Rising's aspirations for economic expansion vaporized because the settlers were not self-supporting; there were too many people, too few houses, and an inadequacy of food and clothing. He was forced to trade with a merchant from Hartford, Connecticut, for grain, fish, salt, bread, cloth, and other needed merchandise. The Lenape on the Schuylkill refused to supply corn because they feared catching the disease that they saw hovering like an evil spirit around the *Örn*. Rising had to send the company's sloop to New England to obtain food, and he also sent the sloop to the Hoerekill and the Appoquinimink to obtain corn and deer meat from the natives.

Through the influence of his assistant commissary, Jacob Swensson, who was highly regarded by the Indians, ten or twelve Lenape chiefs from Passayunk agreed to meet with Rising at Printzhoff. Rising reassured them that the Swedes meant them no harm and that they should trust in God, as the Swedes did, to halt the sickness. Bonds of friendship were renewed, and the chiefs agreed to supply corn to help feed the colonists. As a token of friendship, Rising was obliged to give each sachem a yard of cloth, a kettle, an axe, a hoe, a knife, six awl points, one pound of gunpowder, and one stick of lead for moulding bullets for hunting. About twenty of the Indian camp followers who tagged along with the chiefs had to be given presents, too, and the whole delegation was entertained with an unspecified quantity of "strong drink," which they all enjoyed.

Confirming treaties or land sales with other chiefs at the Hoerekill and in New Jersey required additional quantities of trade goods. Those conferences reduced the inventory intended to buy pelts, and the fur trade consequently suffered. Having also used merchandise brought on the *Örn* to buy necessities from English merchants, Rising had difficulty obtaining goods for the *Örn* to carry back to Sweden, and he knew how costly it was for a vessel to return with an empty hold. He was able to negotiate with another English merchant named Isaac Allerton for 15,926 pounds of Virginia tobacco at nine Stivers per pound, paid for largely on promissory notes. The tobacco filled only forty-seven barrels, not nearly enough to cover the cost of the ship's passage back home, but it was the maximum credit Allerton could extend.

Rising was not only disappointed in the unsatisfactory returns from the colony, he was also forced to deal with the annoyances of English political rivals. Officials from the New Haven colony continued to claim ownership of lands in the Delaware valley, while at the same time the provincial government of Maryland maintained that the land in New Sweden along the west bank of the Delaware south of present Philadelphia belonged to Lord Baltimore by right of the charter Charles I had issued to him. Representatives from Maryland visited Fort Christina to argue for their rights, and the governor of New Haven wrote protesting letters, all of which Rising refuted by arguing that the Swedes possessed legal title by right of land purchase from the rightful Indian owners. The English were fully cognizant of the economic and military weaknesses in the Swedish colony, which obviously diluted Rising's bargaining position. Yet Rising took a strong, positive stand that the Swedish government would fully support him with men and supplies. At the same time he was deeply worried about why the *Haj* had not arrived.

In mid-August a number of soldiers asked Rising for their

release because the limited food supply was being rationed, their linen shirts were worn out, and the supply of coarse sail cloth used as a substitute was exhausted. Strong persuasion was required to convince them not to desert the colony. Rising reminded them that at any day the *Haj* would arrive with supplies. Then on September 24 Rising experienced the heaviest blow since his arrival almost five months earlier; the friendly English merchant from Hartford brought him both good news and bad news from New Amsterdam. The long-awaited *Haj* had arrived with a year's supply of rations for the Swedes—but Director Stuyvesant, piqued at Rising's capture of Fort Casimir, seized the ship and cargo! After confiscating and selling the food, Stuyvesant impressed the vessel in the service of the West India Company and gave it a new name. The crew was disbanded, and the Swedish passengers were put ashore on Manhattan Island, where most of them remained.

A merchant named Hendrick Van Elswick, who was in command of the *Haj,* made his way overland to the Delaware, arriving on November 30 in the company of Lieutenant Swen Höök, a servant, a clerk, and a soldier. Van Elswick and Höök were valuable additions to the staff at Fort Christina. Van Elswick was placed in charge of the storehouse in the fort and the account books, but he could do little that winter to satisfy the widespread hunger in the colony. The situation was worsened by terrible weather. Ice floes in the rivers and creeks damaged houses and boats, and high waters tore the company's sloop loose from her anchor and carried the vessel far up the Christina Kill. Rising himself fell ill with a high fever, and during his illness there were more desertions. To make matters worse, when spring came the winter wheat crop did not mature satisfactorily because of the severity of the weather.

After his "winter of discontent" Rising might have been expected to become discouraged to the point of resigning his frustrating position, but he remained optimistic about the colony and its future. The farm fields were replanted; food, supplies, sheep, and cattle in limited quantity were obtained from merchants in Connecticut and Virginia. Rising had no merchandise

ARTIST'S INTERPRETATION OF
AN EARLY SWEDISH-FINN HOMESTEAD
IN NEW SWEDEN

IN THE FOREGROUND A
LOG DUGOUT IS BEING
HOLLOWED OUT WITH
A HAND ADZ. A KOTA,
WHICH IS TENT SHAPE
IS USED TO STORE ITEMS
OUT OF THE WEATHER.
IN THE DISTANCE LAND
THAT IS UNCLEARED HAS
HAD THE LARGE TREES
FELLED AND THE WHOLE
AREA BURNED.

N. SAWIN

to exchange nor cash to pay for the supplies, but as an economist he knew the procedure of initiating drafts drawn on the Commercial College with the backing of the Swedish government. Of course, he had no direct contact with Sweden because no Swedish vessels arrived; he conducted the negotiations through a factor employed by the New Sweden Company in Holland. The drafts were forwarded to the factor on friendly vessels, and he, in turn, made the necessary arrangements in Stockholm for payments to be made in London and credited to the accounts of the English merchants in America.

For many months the officials of the Commercial College had no way of knowing that the *Haj* had not arrived in New Sweden. They were unaware of the critical need for food and clothing in the colony. Although plans were being made for the continued support of the colony, with the full approval of Charles X, there seemed to be no urgency in preparing a vessel for the crossing. Then on February 16, 1655, a letter Rising had written on September 23, 1654, reached Stockholm reporting the tragedy that had befallen the *Haj*. Preparations for the new expedition were accelerated, and a Dutch-made vessel, the *Mercurius*, was purchased in Saardam, renovated, rerigged, and dispatched to Gothenburg, where preparations were made for the voyage. Rising did not know that sailors were being hired and settlers recruited for an expedition coming to his relief, but with the cooperation of freemen, soldiers, and company employees who remained steadfast in their loyalty to him, he made the most of the situation, confident of the future. There is no clear picture of how much land the settlers were able to bring under the plow or how they managed to survive, but only the hard work and determination of the hardy farm families kept the colony from extinction.

Article 6 of Rising's instructions from the Commercial College told him to "strive to extend the limits of the country," and a significant event complying with those instructions occurred at Fort Christina on June 6-7, 1655, when Jacob Swensson returned from the Susquehanna country with four friendly Minquas chiefs. On behalf of their tribal council the chiefs presented land to Rising on the east side of the Elk River "from the beginning of the Chakakitque-fall all the way unto the ends of Amisackan-fall . . . a land of choice soil endowed with beautiful fresh rivers, so that many thousand families, who might settle there can find nourishment." The Minquas were not altruistic in making the gift because they stipulated that the Swedes should build trading posts on the land and keep them well supplied with European merchandise for their convenience. The Swedes were also to settle blacksmiths and gunsmiths at the trading posts to mend Indian guns.

Rising was very pleased with the proposition and agreed to take full advantage of it as soon as Swedish ships arrived with reinforcements and goods. Although it is difficult to bound this land with precision, it substantially added to the physical size of New Sweden by extending the western boundary. It meant there would be plenty of fertile land to accomodate all the Swedes who wanted to come to America, and by positioning their trading posts in former Minquas territory, the Swedes would have preference over both the English and the Dutch in their commerce with the Susquehanna Indians.

What do we know about those freemen, soldiers, servants, and company employees who remained loyal to Director Rising and were willing to endure the hardships in the colony? In the aggregate they represented persons who had crossed the Atlantic at different times, some having come on the *Örn* with Rising and others with Printz. A number came on one of the *Kalmar Nyckel*'s three voyages, or on one of the several other Swedish vessels. Among the most common of the male personal names were Anders, Hendrick, Lars, Johan, Mats, Peter, Sven, and some of the family names were patronyms, which means they were derived from the father's Christian name. Anders, a son of Sven, might be called Anders Svensson; and Johan, a son of Anders Svensson, could be known as Johan Andersson. The patronymic then became a family name, and Svensson was modified to Swanson; Johan Andersson was anglicized to John Anderson. In some instances an individual appended an alias to his name; one of the Johan Anderssons added Stålfkota ("steel jacket'') to his name to distinguish him from others of the same name. That addition evolved into a family name variously rendered as Staelcop, Stalcop, or Stalcup. Other examples could be cited of how surnames were adopted by the early Swedish-Americans—some based on a trade or profession, others on a town of one's origin—and how those names supplanted the patronym.

Those men, as well as the women and children, cross the pages of Delaware valley history as faceless characters. They lived in an age before cameras were invented and in a colony where there were no portrait painters. Portraits of some of the aristocrats and nobles, like Johan Printz, Axel Oxenstierna, Per Brahe, and others were executed in Sweden, but no paintings or drawings of the ordinary people who came to America are known to exist. The tendency is to visualize them as blue-eyed, fair-skinned people descended from sea-roving Norsemen. Many may have met that description, but there must also have been brunettes with brown eyes and redheads with hazel eyes of the same physical type seen today on the streets of Stockholm or Gothenburg. There were Germans, Dutch, Holsteiners, and other nationalities; some may have been tall, others short; some wore beards, others did not; some were bald, and others had hair hanging almost to their shoulders. At least one of them was the black man from West Africa who was working with other laborers in 1644 cutting hay in the fields at Printzhoff and serving as a deckhand on Governor Printz's sloop. His name is among those listed on the official rolls as gunners, trumpeters, blacksmiths, carpenters, swineherders, drummers, soldiers, gunsmiths, farm hands, clerks, maid servants, etc.

There was no continuity in the enrollment lists, and Anthony, the black man, vanishes from the records after 1654 along with many others. No one can be certain what happened to them. The lineage of many others can be traced through birth, marriage, and death records. Today there are innumerable descendants of those early Scandinavians living not only in the Delaware valley but throughout the United States. One thing about their ancestors is certain: the early Swedes and Finns were not a light-hearted people moved by frivolity. The reader has seen that some of them were forcibly recruited for service in New Sweden in lieu of punishment at home. On at least one occasion a discredited soldier was exiled to the colony for life. That aspect of the migration should not be exaggerated, because there were many who came of their own accord. However, whether one came voluntarily or involuntarily, it was not a pleasure cruise, because the colonists faced privation, even death, during the voyage and an unknown future when they reached their destination. The faces of both men and women alike must have reflected to some degree the tense, realistic outlook on life that daily toil in a new land demanded of them.

Once the Scandinavian immigrant came ashore at Fort Christina, where practically all of them disembarked, he began the struggle to keep himself and his family alive. Some kind of shelter had to be found; fields cleared and cultivated; seeds of various grains planted, harvested, and thrashed; and gardens dug to raise vegetable for the family's survival. Too much rain or too little rain affected the crops adversely, and overexposure in uncertain weather aggravated malnutrition, fevers, and undiagnosed ailments. The Lenape Indian who was friendly one day could be unintentionally provoked by the actions of a neighbor or official and become a treacherous enemy the next. There were predatory animals and poisonous snakes in the woods, and blood-hungry swarms of mosquitos breeding in the marshland on either side of the tributaries emptying into the Delaware.

The quest for survival left no time for painting, music, literature, or other forms of artistic expression; in fact, the Scandinavian peasant farmers brought very little esthetic tradition to the New World. There are no references in the records of New Sweden to dancing, frolics, quilting bees, or social gatherings to enliven what, according to modern standards, would be described as a life with a minimum of leisure and few sources of amusement. There must have been storytelling, possibly folk dances, and periods of fun; one assumes that the children must have been taught games that were played in the homeland, but specific details are lacking.

Hymn and psalm-singing during religious services provided some relaxation, but there were no organs or other instrumental accompaniment to the singing such as fiddling, to the best of our knowledge. In the absence of music the repetition of memorized verses was probably not sparked by evangelical emotion; the people who were illiterate had to be taught by rote. Although they all may have taken their Lutheran faith seriously, religion appears to have been more of a duty than an expression of thoughtful devotion. In most cases religious attendance was compulsory; Peter Minuit was instructed to levy a fine of six Stivers on any sailor or soldier absent from morning prayers on the first crossing of the *Kalmar Nyckel*. Printz demanded attendance at church services or at the services conducted by lay readers among those who lived too far away to attend the church at Tinicum or the chapel at Fort Christina. Rising was ordered to "see to it that diligent religious services" were conducted.

Formal church services, with responsive readings, prayers, songs, lengthy sermons, periodically followed by Holy Communion, were held every Wednesday, Friday, and twice on Sunday. Religious holidays such as New Years, Pentecost, Epiphany, Candlemas Day, Day of Annunciation, John the Baptist's Day, Good Friday, Easter, Ascension Day, Saint Michael's Day, All Saint's Day, and Christmas were faithfully observed. It was obligatory for families to attend services and refrain from work or worldly pursuits on holy days.

The caliber of the preaching must have been mediocre, for Rising wrote in his 1654 report that, "We are in need of a learned priest, although we now have three of them." He said that one of them, Pastor Hiört, was "both materially and spiritually a poor priest." Obviously there were competent ministers in Sweden, but the colony did not get the best ones. Perhaps the most scholarly theologian sent to New Sweden was Johan Campanius, but he was only paid ten Riksdalers a month, which he had to supplement by farming and raising cows to support his large family. He remained only five years because, as he wrote, "I am too weary to endure it longer in these parts."

References have been made in previous chapters to log houses and log churches, but what has not been emphasized is that the log cabin made its American debut with the Swedes and Finns in the Delaware valley. Log cabins were not built by English colonists who settled Virginia, Maryland, and New England, nor by the Dutch in New York. Homes of horizontally-placed round or hewn logs, held together not by nails but by interlocking corners, were not part of the architectural heritage of England or Holland. Settlers from those countries built crude houses of clapboards, bricks, stone, boards, studs, and clay, patterned after their European homes. Sometimes they imitated the Indian bark wigwam as a temporary shelter.

Log structures were an integral part of the folkways in rural Sweden and Finland, where the people were attuned to a forest environment. They brought to America the kind of vernacular log-house techniques with which they were familiar. Later German and Swiss immigrants also brought to the Delaware valley the log-building techniques used in their homeland.

As young America expanded, Scotch-Irish immigrants, and those of other nationalities, borrowed the log-cabin concepts of the Germanic peoples. The pioneer log cabin became the typical frontier dwelling. The earliest log cabins, those first built by the Swedes and Finns, were devoid of glass windows, having sliding wood coverings in lieu of sashes and panes. The chimney appended to the exterior of the cabin was sometimes made of field stones but more often of tree limbs and mud daub, a so-called "catted chimney" like that depicted on the cabin of Abraham Lincoln. No bricks were made in New Sweden up to and through the Rising administration, and no brick houses were built during that same period. The limited quantities of bricks brought over from Sweden were used in fireplaces, ovens, and chimneys in homes like Printzhoff and those occupied by officers within the forts.

The Swedish and Finnish farmers did not build large barns, like those later built by Pennsylvania-German farmers, for use as shelter for cows and horses as well as storage quarters for hay, grains, plows, and farm tools. Daniel Pastorius, a German, commented in 1684 that the Scandinavians "allow their cattle,

LOG CABINS: BUILT BY THE FIRST SWEDES AND FINNS AS THE ARTIST VISUALIZES THEM. THEY WERE BUILT CLOSE TO THE CREEKS—ALL TRIBUTARIES OF THE DELAWARE RIVER

THE KOTAS WERE BUILT FOR TEMPORARY SHELTER POSTS MADE FROM SMALL TREES LAID IN TEEPEE FORM WERE COVERED WITH BARK AND TURF.

LOG SHED

horses, cows, swine, etc., to run in the woods summer and winter.'' That was only partially true, because many Swedish and Finnish farmers, who allowed pigs and hogs to forage unattended in the woods, built pens and fences of split log rails to keep sheep, goats, and cattle from gardens and cultivated fields. There is a record of a log stable at Fort Christina, probably to house horses and oxen, and some farmers owning a horse or two may have built small stables. Sheds built of notched logs were found on most farms; they were used for granaries and other storage purposes.

Both Swedes and Finns erected a specialized one-room log bath house, known to the Swedes as a badstu and to the Finns as a sauna, usually near a running stream. Water was poured over stones heated in the interior fireplace to make steam that enveloped the nude bathers. During exposure to the steam bath they whipped their bodies with switches of twigs to stimulate circulation. After exposure to the steam in the bath house, the bathers, glistening with perspiration, dashed out and plunged into the cold creek water. Members of a family often took the sweat bath together, sometimes in the company of invited friends or relatives, in both winter and summer alike. ''A Swedish bath,'' wrote Christopher Ward, a former president of the Historical Society of Delaware, ''was at once a hygenic exercise, a social function, and a valorous deed!''

Before there were blacksmiths in the colony everything of metal had to be imported, including axes, adzes, spades, sickles, knives, chisels, handsaws, awls, and gimlets. Guns and ammunition, copper and iron kettles, plowshares, and hoes were also brought from Europe. When blacksmiths arrived they beat red-hot iron bars on their anvils to make tools for those freemen who could afford to pay. Since Swedish money was scarce, blacksmiths and other craftsmen were paid in sewant, tobacco, beaver pelts, or other negotiable commodities. The company extended credit terms to its own employees, and books were kept to record debits and credits so that appropriate adjustments could be made in an individual's wages. Very little money actually exchanged hands in the colony. Even freemen not on the company's payroll bought products from the storehouse at Fort Christina in exchange for certain services, farm products, or pelts.

Unusual negotiations had to be made from time to time. For example, the company owned cattle, and several head were loaned to the freemen who arrived with Rising so that they "could make a start" at farming. In return the settlers agreed to turn over a certain part of their produce to the company. Cows were portioned out to other settlers on a rental basis that called for an annual payment of a certain quantity of butter and half of the animal's offspring. During Rising's administration very little tobacco was grown in the colony, the colonists preferring to raise edibles. Minuit's ambition to make New Sweden an important tobacco-growing colony never materialized.

Through necessity many of the Scandinavian farmers resorted to their own ingenuity and skill to make implements and utensils of wood using hand tools. Wood carving was well developed in Swedish folk crafts dating back to prehistoric times, the forests supplying an abundance of raw material. Trees to the colonists in New Sweden were not prized for shade, shelter, or beauty; they were a source of edible nuts and fruits and a natural resource that could be converted into cabins, fences, and numerous useful things.

Swedish and Finnish-American farmers used trees to make the furniture for their cabins: benches, stools, tables, chests, and sleeping bunks. Plates, bowls, spoons, ladles, pails, and churns were all fashioned from wood. Although Rising visualized pottery makers working in the colony, that never became a reality. There was neither a pottery nor a glass industry in New Sweden, which resulted in further dependence upon wood. Harrows, rakes, and hay forks of wood were made by the self-sufficient craftsmen as a substitute for those made of metal.

A sled-like conveyance of wood used to pull heavy loads was harnessed to a horse or ox with thongs of twisted strips of deerskin instead of scarce ropes and chains. Horses and oxen were also used to plow the fields, and, if necessary, a resourceful Scandinavian farmer could make a wooden plow. In the

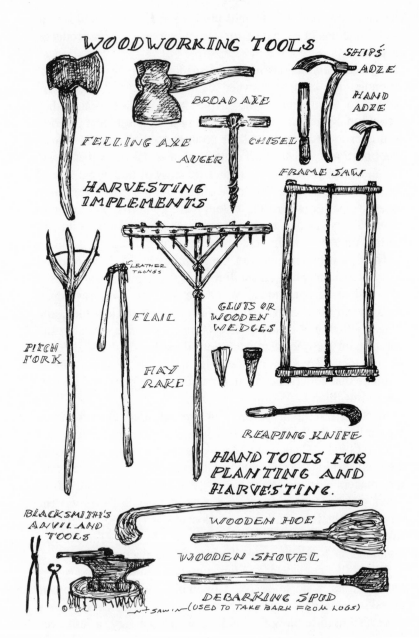

WOODWORKING TOOLS

SHIPS ADZE

BROAD AXE

HAND ADZE

FELLING AXE

CHISEL

AUGER

FRAME SAW

HARVESTING IMPLEMENTS

LEATHER THONGS

GLUTS OR WOODEN WEDGES

PITCH FORK

FLAIL

HAY RAKE

REAPING KNIFE

HAND TOOLS FOR PLANTING AND HARVESTING.

BLACKSMITH'S ANVIL AND TOOLS

WOODEN HOE

WOODEN SHOVEL

DEBARKING SPUD (USED TO TAKE BARK FROM LOGS)

absence of roads there was little need for wagons. Land travel was mostly on foot over narrow Indian paths, but walking was tiresome and often dangerous. The best and safest routes were the rivers and navigable creeks, which is an important reason why the log dwellings were strung out along the waterways where the fertile soil was conducive to farming. Some craftsmen constructed wooden rowboats; others built dugout canoes, a traditional form in Scandinavia similar to that used by the Lenape. Those canoes were not made of birchbark but were simply hollowed-out logs propelled by long poles or paddles.

Families tended to be large, because sons and daughters were a useful asset in the fields and household. Boys aided their fathers outdoors, and daughters assisted their mothers with cooking, churning, butter and cheesemaking, washing, spinning, sewing, weaving, and many other chores. Thus, the traditional craft skills which were part of Scandinavian culture were passed along to the new generation and augmented by certain traits borrowed from the Indians.

Large quantities of duffel cloth, frieze, and linens were brought by ship from Sweden, but during the periods when no vessels arrived the cloth was exhausted in the storehouse in Fort Christina. Sometimes the commissaries negotiated purchases from Dutch and English merchants for cloth used to make badly needed dresses, aprons, shirts, underclothing, and other garments. Although no cotton was raised in the colony, many families owned a few head of sheep that were sheared periodically, and the Swedish women were familiar with the use of the spinning wheel. They knitted woolen stockings, mittens, shawls, and scarves, although records of ships' cargoes indicate that consignments of felt, woolen, and linen stockings for both men and women were brought from Sweden.

Quantities of shoes were also received on some of the ships, insufficient, to be sure, for permanent accomodation in a land where shoes were exposed to heavy wear. It seems likely that some families could not afford to pay the colony's shoemakers for conventional shoes, those with leather tops and soles and heels of wood, and had to resort to duplicating Indian moccassins.

Deerskin was also used to make jackets when cloth coats were unavailable or too expensive to be bought from a tailor. Elkskin was widely used to make men's trousers, and animal-skin turbans probably replaced the cloth hats and caps brought from Sweden when they wore out.

Farmers raised chickens in limited numbers, as well as the goats, pigs, and sheep already mentioned. Cows, oxen, and horses were not plentiful, and such enterprises as dairy farms or cattle ranches were nonexistent in an economy that consisted of small family farms. Each household raised its own edibles, supplemented by hunting, fishing, and gathering. Pork, venison, fowl, and fish were staple foods; peas, beans, cabbages, and turnips were the most common vegetables. Most of the farms had peach and other fruit trees, and members of the family also picked wild grapes, which grew abundantly and were a real treat to Scandinavians coming from an area where grapes were less plentiful. Various species of native berries and edible nuts were also plentiful in the woods.

Rye, wheat, and corn flour were used in baking bread. Some farmers took their grist to be ground at the mill on Cobbs Creek or to the windmill at Fort Christina when it was operative, but many used home hand mills or querns. Hand mills were made of two stones roughly circular in shape, the lower one held stationary and the top one turned by hand; the grain was crushed between them.

Hops and barley were raised for brewing strong beer, not iced but served at room temperature and consumed by adults and children alike. Tea and coffee were apparently not served in the early days of the colony. Wines and distilled liquors like brandy and rum were imported from Sweden, or obtained from English or Dutch merchants. Demand exceeded the limited supply. Probably some of the colonists made their own berry or wild grape wine for use on festive occasions.

Corn was an indigenous American plant that most of the Scandinavian farmers saw for the first time growing in the Indian fields, and they soon learned to plant, cultivate, and harvest their own crops. Their wives borrowed corn recipes from the Indian women, such as roasting ears, succotash, hominy, ash cake, and corn pone. They learned to plait the corn husks to make doormats and seat coverings. Corn husks were also used as stuffing for mattresses, although geese, duck, chicken feathers, and straw were all used for the same purpose. The Indians taught the Swedes how to use native gourds as dippers, water bottles, and containers and how to make fish nets of vines or plaited grass. The Indian women wove baskets from grass, reeds, oak splints, and corn husks that they used for storing or carrying corn, beans, berries, nuts, and fruits. The Scandinavian women were familiar with bark baskets in their homeland, and they had no difficulty in applying their native techniques to the materials available to them.

The women cooked food over an open fireplace, usually built in the corner of a Swedish-Finnish log cabin. The fireplace was a cook stove and an oven, a furnace during the winter, and, to some extent, a source of light after sundown. Candles made of tallow, beeswax, or bayberries were also used for light as were long splinters of resinous pine stuck into the crevices in the interior log walls. Both candles and splints were short-lived and were used sparingly because of their value. Whale oil was used in lamps in Sweden, as were candles, but whale oil was a rare commodity in New Sweden. The family found it practical to go to bed shortly after sundown to conserve light and heat. During the cold weather the bedding in the cabins consisted mostly of deerskin, bearskin, and other animal furs, although some families must have treasured the well-worn blankets they had brought from the ''old country'' and used aboard ship during the crossing on cold nights. Those blankets, like the tin goblets and tin dishes they also brought with them, became heirlooms, the last ties with the material culture of the homeland.

In the cramped quarters of the log cabin home, the Swedish wife had to do almost everything by hand, from salting pork and curing bacon to making jellies and preserves and baking bread. She had to learn which wild American herbs could be safely picked for seasoning, which were poisonous, and which could be used for medicinal purposes. She had to treat the children's

INSIDE THE LOG CABIN

FIRE PLACES WERE IN THE CORNER. EARLY FLOORS
WERE DIRT — LATER PUNCHEONS WERE USED. (SPLIT LOGS
WITH FLAT END UP.) BEDS WERE MADE OF LOGS OR
PUNCHEONS. FEATHERS, SKINS, AND LOCAL
GRASSES WERE USED AS MATTRESSES. MOST
KITCHEN UTENSILS AND FURNITURE WERE MADE OF
                                    WOOD.

ailments, dress burns and cuts, prepare poultices and balms for external application to cure croup and cramps, and bring relief to aching muscles. Above all, she had to be prepared to deliver her own infant, with the assistance of a midwife, a daughter, or a neighbor woman.

8. THE FALL OF NEW SWEDEN

Stuyvesant received the welcome news at New Amsterdam on July 16, 1654, that peace had been agreed upon between England and the Netherlands; Rising learned about it shortly thereafter at Fort Christina. Rising must have realized that since Stuyvesant no longer had reason to fear an attack from New England, the time was ripe for him to turn his attention to the Swedes at Fort Trinity.

Stuyvesant had been smarting since the day he received a letter from Rising, written a week after the latter's arrival in New Sweden and carried to New Amsterdam by a freeman named Peter Jochimsson, who was accompanied by an Indian guide. Rising said in his letter that he had arrived from Sweden with a goodly number of people and had "in the name of Her Royal Majesty of Sweden, my most gracious Queen, summoned the fort erected at the Sand point, which after exclusion of further delay was voluntarily surrendered with the adjoining Colonists, who learning the reasonable conditions offered them, together with the liberty of going or remaining, repaired under the obedience of Her Royal Majesty aforesaid, and afterwards took the oath of allegiance and fidelity at our hands."

Rising was on a collision course and did not seem to realize it. No matter how he had occupied Fort Casimir—by aggression, argument, or compromise—he should have known his letter would antagonize Stuyvesant. To tell a proud rival you have "summoned" his country's property and caused his followers to take an oath of obedience, does not seem to be a way to initiate harmonious relations. Stuyvesant did not answer the letter. Instead he wrote to his superiors in Holland to advise them that a new Swedish governor had insulted both the West India Company and the Dutch government by seizing the Dutch fort at the Santhoeck and confiscating the adjacent property. Rising, who held to the notion that the difference between the Dutch and the Swedes could be peacefully resolved through diplomatic channels, was unaware of Stuyvesant's letter or the reaction of the directors, who considered him guilty of an unpardonable sin that had to be severely punished. They wrote Stuyvesant ordering him to drive the Swedes out of the Delaware River valley by force and to restrict occupation there exclusively to the Dutch. After further consideration cooler heads prevailed, and they wrote a second letter modifying the first that instructed Stuyvesant to invade New Sweden but to allow the Swedes to retain ownership of Fort Christina and the contiguous land provided they "shall consider themselves subjects of this State and the Company."

It did not take long for news to reach Rising that Stuyvesant was making preparations to come to the Delaware River, although the details of his mission were vague. Rising concluded that Stuyvesant's sole objective was to reclaim Fort Trinity, not necessarily by military action, but possibly through arbitration with him. He still did not know that the West India Company, which strongly influenced Dutch international policies, had decreed that the Swedish threat had to be removed once and for all from New Netherland. The time seemed propitious to the directors, because Charles X had taken Sweden to war against Poland. The Swedish king was so involved in battles and sieges that it was unlikely he would turn against Holland because of an incident on the other side of the Atlantic involving only a handful of his subjects.

While Rising was trying to second-guess Stuyvesant's intentions, the Dutch governor and his council, with the company's authorization, were impressing suitable ships anchored in the New Amsterdam harbor into an attack force. The company compensated their owners or captains, and a provincial commissioner, Foppe Jansen Outhout, was appointed to make certain the flotilla was well supplied with guns, ammunition, and victuals. The principal vessel was a large warship owned by the City of Amsterdam called the *Wagh* (meaning *Scales* or *Balance*), which the city's burgomasters chartered for use in the company's service. Commanded by Captain Frederick de Coningh (also spelled Coninck), the *Wagh* carried thirty-six cannon. While it was on loan to the company, Captain Coningh was instructed to take his orders from Stuyvesant and his council.

Six other vessels were made ready to join the *Wagh*.* Four were identified as yachts—a loose term that did not conform to the modern concept of a pleasure yacht—the *Holland Garden*, *Princess Royal*, *Dolphin*, and *Abraham's Offering*. The fifth, the *Love*, was known as a flyboat, and the sixth, named *Hope*, was called a galiot. Each vessel was armed with at least four cannon, although the firepower of the *Wagh* was in excess of the six vessels combined and sufficient to smash Fort Trinity's defenses by itself.

Various figures were recorded as to the size of the attacking force. Lindeström estimated there were 1500 men; Skute said there were 800; and Rising calculated the Dutch strength at 600 or 700. Those figures are probably all exaggerated. Stuyvesant said there were fifty or sixty seamen on the *Wagh* and forty soldiers, and that 150–160 militiamen were distributed among the other smaller craft, making an approximate total of 250. That was probably an understatement, because attackers and defenders alike tend to use figures that put themselves in the best light.

A Dutch civilian named Johannes Bogaert, who was aboard the *Wagh* and who had no reason to underestimate or overestimate, took a head count. He recorded in a letter that the forces "consisted of 317 soldiers besides a company of sailors." He noted that the soldiers were divided into six separate companies, and he specifically gave the number of men in each company, which ranged from fifty to ninety, as well as the names of the company commanders who served under General Stuyvesant

---

*This is the Swedish spelling. The Dutch word was *Waegh*.

and Vice-Governor Nicasius de Sille, a member of the council who accompanied the expedition.

In the earlier invasion of New Sweden in 1651, Stuyvesant had acted without the knowledge or consent of the company's directors, a fact that prompted him to exercise caution to avoid creating an incident that would provoke a confrontation with the Swedish government. The second time, having the full support and encouragement of his superiors and written orders to subdue the Swedes, he felt free to proceed with less restraint. On the other hand, Stuyvesant was neither reckless nor unChristian, and he did not want to be responsible for unnecessary bloodshed.

The flotilla sailed from New Amsterdam on September 5 by the Dutch calendar, which was ten days ahead of the Swedish calendar, a disparity that must be kept in mind when one contrasts the Swedish and Dutch versions of the assault. According to the Swedish calendar Rising gives August 30 as the date the Dutch fleet arrived and anchored on the east side of the Delaware opposite the ruins of Fort Elfsborg. Although Rising had hopes of a peaceful negotiation, he decided to prepare for the worst. He concentrated his military strength at Fort Trinity under command of Captain Sven Skute, assisted by Lieutenant Gyllengren, Ensign Peter Wendell, and Peter Lindeström. He supplied the fort with forty-seven bushels of rye (probably to be used in baking bread), fourteen gallons of brandy, a quantity of beer, and other provisions and materiel. He transferred 150 pounds of gunpowder from Fort Christina, along with muskets, swords, pikes, bullets, and some of his best soldiers. The exact number of men that made up the garrison at Fort Trinity is not known, but there were at least forty or fifty. The reduced garrison at Fort Christina was commanded by Van Elswick, with Lieutenant Höök second in command. Both were competent men, but in retrospect it appears that Rising may have erred in strengthening Fort Trinity at the expense of Fort Christina, because he did not anticipate that Stuyvesant would attack the latter post, a serious miscalculation on his part.

Prior to the arrival of the Dutch flotilla, Rising conferred with his officers, and with their agreement he prepared a written resolution for Skute's guidance. Skute was instructed that when the Dutch ships appeared in the river he should send out a party in a small boat to board the principal ship and ask if the Dutch came on a friendly mission. If so, he was supposed to arrange for a peaceful discussion between the Dutch and Swedish governors about bounds and territories. Skute was told that if the Dutch refused to negotiate he should stand firm and not allow their vessels to sail past the fort "upon pain of being fired upon, which in such case they could not reckon [it] an act of hostility." This seeming paradox meant that the Dutch failure to negotiate could be blamed for forcing the Swedes to protect themselves, and the Dutch, not the Swedes, would then be guilty of a hostile act. Of course, Stuyvesant never intended to negotiate with the Swedes, and that was Rising's second miscalculation.

On the morning of August 31, according to the Swedish calendar, which will be used below, the Dutch flotilla crossed the river diagonally from the site of the former Fort Elfsborg to the present New Castle shore "amidst the beating of drums and the blowing of trumpets and a great bravado," according to Lindeström's account. No shots were fired as the vessels, moving northerly close to the shoreline, passed in front of Fort Trinity. For some unexplained reason, Skute did not send out a party to board the *Wagh*, as ordered. One by one the Dutch ships passed by and anchored a short distance north of the fort, where the troops landed and began to construct breastworks. Stuyvesant's plans were to consolidate his forces and attack the fort by land on the northside, his eastern flank protected by the vessels at anchor in the river. Having built the fort, Stuyvesant knew the terrain, and his force included some men who had formerly lived at the Santhoeck.

Rising was not at Fort Trinity when the Dutch vessels passed; he was either at Fort Christina or in his recently built dwelling on nearby Timber Island. He later wrote bitterly that Skute "suffered the Dutch ships to pass the fort without remonstrance or firing a gun," which he felt was reprehensible. Lindeström, who was at Fort Trinity as the Dutch ships passed, later accused

Skute of traitorous conduct in not offering resistance. Although Lindeström admitted that some of Skute's soldiers were cowardly and insubordinate, he—and Lieutenant Gyllengren—believed that Skute was too willing to surrender to Stuyvesant even before an attack began.

The position on the shore taken by Stuyvesant's soldiers effectively cut the lines of communication between Fort Trinity and Fort Christina, and Skute was unable to confer with Rising. Skute came out of the fort to the Dutch camp twice under a flag of truce, and on the first visit requested permission to send an open letter to Rising, a request Stuyvesant firmly rejected. In the meantime, the Dutch were strengthening their beachhead, and Skute came to the Dutch position for a second time. Lindeström wrote that he watched the proceedings through a telescope, and when Skute met Stuyvesant "he fell upon his knees and begged for pardon." Lindeström may have been prejudiced against Skute, but the fact remains that shortly thereafter Skute went aboard the *Wagh* with Stuyvesant, where they both signed surrender terms on September 1.

A detailed account of Skute's surrender is discussed in my book *Swedes and Dutch At New Castle*, and further repetition seems unnecessary. The important thing is that Skute acquiesced to the surrender terms, not Rising, who is often blamed for the loss of Fort Trinity but who was not even there. After Stuyvesant and Skute agreed on the conditions of surrender, Stuyvesant moved his command post to the fort, restoring the name Fort Casimir and running up the Dutch colors. He held Skute and the other Swedish officers under temporary arrest, although he did not jail them. They were treated as officers and gentlemen, and accepted Stuyvesant's invitation to dine with him at his own table. This considerate treatment was not accorded thirty of the common soldiers in the Swedish garrison; they were imprisoned as prisoners of war, placed aboard the ship *Love,* and forcibly taken to New Amsterdam. Thus Rising lost their assistance at Fort Christina when he needed it most.

Rising's first indication of Skute's surrender was when the Dutch vessels in the river celebrated the victory by firing their cannon. That was a signal the fort was lost, but Rising still seemed uncertain of Stuyvesant's motives. He sent Van Elswick to Fort Casimir to confer with Stuyvesant and "to obtain an explanation of his arrival and intention, and to dissuade him from further hostilities, as we could not be persuaded that he seriously purposed to disturb us in the lawful dominion of His Royal Majesty and our principles."

Stuyvesant insisted that the Swedes were trespassing on Dutch territory. He told Van Elswick that he intended to take and hold what belonged to the West India Company. When Van Elswick returned with Stuyvesant's answer, Rising put his men to work, by night and day, in an attempt to secure the ramparts and gabions at Fort Christina. It might be argued that Rising's best defensive tactics, when he first learned that Stuyvesant was coming to New Sweden, would have been to vacate Fort Trinity and concentrate his manpower, armaments, and supplies at Fort Christina. Then when he learned of Stuyvesant's determination to use force instead of arbitration he would have been better prepared to withstand a siege at Fort Christina for a longer period of time. As it turned out, both forts were lost at the outset due to insufficient manpower. If the garrison had been strong enough to hold out for a week longer Stuyvesant would have been forced to give up the assault. Events were developing in New Amsterdam, as the reader will shortly see, that would have prevented Stuyvesant from sustaining a siege at Fort Christina.

Having miscalculated Stuyvesant's intent, Rising's surrender of Fort Christina was inevitable because he could not hold out long enough in a position he had deliberately weakened. The day after Fort Trinity fell, Dutch soldiers appeared on the southwest bank of the Christina immediately opposite Fort Christina to examine the terrain and select suitable emplacements where they could install their batteries. They were plainly visible from the fort, and Rising sent Lieutenant Höök and a drummer in a small boat to ask them what they were doing there. This was a superfluous question to ask of soldiers whose commander had sent a message back with Van Elswick that left no doubt as to his intentions. The drummer accompanying an officer on a mission of peace was supposed to beat his drum as a signal that the officer came for a discussion and not to spy on the enemy or cause any harm. Höök's drummer was rowing the boat and couldn't beat his drum at the same time, but Höök called out to the Dutch on shore asking if he could land and talk to them. They answered affirmatively, but when he pulled ashore, he was not accompanied by the beat of a drum; consequently they took him to Stuyvesant at Fort Casimir as a spy.

Rising still could not believe that Stuyvesant was on an attack mission even as the *Wagh* and *Dolphin* sailed into the mouth of the Christina to bottle up the stream and Dutch soldiers appeared in greater numbers on the opposite side of the Christina. Rising wrote that "some of our people interpreted this as indicating the purpose of the Dutch is to be to claim and hold all our territory up to the Creek and construct a fort there. . . ." Since Stuyvesant already possessed the fort that dominated the territory and controlled the Delaware water corridor, why would he want to build another fort?

Johannes Bogaert aboard the *Wagh* and Peter Lindeström at Fort Casimir each described how Stuyvesant deployed his troops as he planned the seige of Fort Christina. In his book *Geographia Americae,* Lindeström included a drawing showing how Stuyvesant's forces virtually surrounded the fort and Christinahamn. The two accounts differ in the number of cannon and other details, but both agree that formidable offensive batteries were established on all sides of the fort and even at Rising's new house on Timber Island, which the Dutch had seized. The superior Dutch armament ranged from cannon shooting three-, six-, and eight-pound balls to larger ones capable of firing twelve and eighteen pounders.

On September 5, Stuyvesant sent an Indian from Fort Casimir with a message for Rising. Its contents were clear and concise, leaving no reason to doubt his objectives. Stuyvesant demanded the surrender not only of Fort Christina but of all New Sweden, and he required the Swedes to evacuate or remain in the colony under Dutch authority. Rising then held a council of war attended by Van Elswick and several other soldiers. His ranking officers, Skute, Gyllengren, Wendel, and Lindeström were still detained at Fort Casimir, and Höök was in prison in the hold of the *Wagh*. They could not participate in the discussion; nevertheless, a decision was made to put up the best defense as long as possible. It was also agreed not to commence or provoke hostilities because of the scarcity of powder, but to wait until the enemy fired on them or began to storm the fort.

Rising answered Stuyvesant's ultimatum with a letter in which he again tried to dissuade the Dutch governor from aggression, repeating that the Swedes were determined to defend their rights to the utmost of their strength and that Stuyvesant would have to answer for the consequences. Stuyvesant replied that he had his orders and that his superiors in Holland who had issued the orders could answer for the consequences. He was determined, as ordered, to possess the whole river. He then proceeded to show that he meant what he said. The attackers so greatly outnumbered the defenders that some of the Dutch troops sailed farther up the Delaware, possibly with the objective of taking Fort New Gothenburg on Tinicum Island, if it were still functionally sound. The records are not clear whether any cannon remained at that fort, or if there were soldiers to fire them, but no engagement was fought there, and New Gothenburg is not mentioned in either the Dutch or Swedish accounts of the invasion.

Who gave the orders to the Dutch troops to loot the houses and farms of the Swedish and Finnish settlers is not known, but the troops raided properties at Marcus Hook, Chester, and elsewhere. Rising wrote that they killed cattle, goats, swine, and poultry, broke open houses, plundering many "and stripped them to the skin." Armegot Printz Papegoja encouraged the families to bring their valuables to Printzhoff, where she evidently thought they would be safe, but Dutch soldiers broke in and stole what they wanted, including her personal belongings. There is no evidence of physical damage inflicted on the colonists nor any record of deaths or serious injuries, although Rising accused the soldiers of shooting horses wantonly, and in the vicinity of Fort Christina "females have been dragged out of their houses by force, whole buildings torn down, even hauled away." Dutch soldiers also burnt the houses at Christinahamn to the ground.

Nothing was said about this rapacious behavior in any of Stuyvesant's letters or reports, but Rising considered it a disgrace for Dutch troops to behave "as if they were in the country of their bitterest enemy." Unfortunately no journals or letters written by Swedish or Finnish victims have yet come to light to tell of their experiences at the hands of the invaders.

In the meantime, the Dutch besieging Fort Christina continued to consolidate their positions, transferring guns and ammunition from the vessels and allocating men to the positions assigned each of the batteries for a coordinated attack when Stuyvesant gave the command. Progress was necessarily slow because of the extensive marshes; small boats were needed to carry men and supplies to fastland where cannon and earthworks could be safely placed. Stuyvesant probably hoped that his display of superiority, which was strengthened almost daily, would demoralize the defenders and that Rising would have no alternative except to capitulate without offering resistance. If so, he was not far from wrong. The defenders in Fort Christina had become tired and worn out; a few were ill; some had deserted. Only thirty remained, according to Rising's account of the "Unexpected and Hostile Attack on the Swedish Colony." Food was scanty, and the supply of powder "scarcely sufficed for a single round of our guns," Rising wrote.

In view of the desperate condition at the fort, Rising decided that it was then timely for him to confer personally with Stuyvesant. Several meetings were held in a "large and beautiful tent" that Stuyvesant's men had erected between the fort and the Dutch lines. Rising gives September 13 as the date of the first meeting attended by himself and Van Elswick on the Swedish side and Stuyvesant and Nicasius de Sille on the Dutch side. It was truly an historic meeting, especially since it may have been the first time the two governors had met in person. Each had already formed an impression of the other through the reports of their subordinates and by the messages they had exchanged. They probably spoke in German or Dutch, because both knew the two languages, and Stuyvesant was not well versed in Swedish. The two protagonists were men of different personalities and backgrounds: Stuyvesant, the soldier, a man of action, an administrator and politician; Rising, a theorist and scholar having limited political experience, and, so far as is known, no field military background.

Stuyvesant was then forty-five years of age, and his likeness, believed to have been executed by the Dutch-American artist Henry Couturier, the Delaware valley's first portrait painter, depicts him as a smooth-shaven, stern-faced man, with an eagle-beak nose, a bald pate, and tresses of long black hair hanging down almost to his shoulders. Rising was only thirty-eight, but no portrait of him is known to exist, and neither his size, his weight, nor his general appearance have been described in the contemporary accounts. Nothing concrete was accomplished in this first meeting, the two men expressing the positions previously taken in their written messages. Rising registered his protests, and Stuyvesant insisted upon the surrender of New Sweden. However, when Rising returned to the fort there was no doubt in his mind that Stuyvesant meant what he said. He had the manpower and weaponry to take what he wanted; the Swedish position was hopeless. Rising knew that offering resistance would be a useless waste of lives.

On September 14 a second meeting was held in the tent. Rising was accompanied by Van Elswick and Jacob Swensson, and Stuyvesant brought de Sille and Captain Frederick Coningh. The conference lasted for about an hour, and tentative articles of capitulation, drawn up by Elswick at Rising's request, were discussed. Probably much to Rising's surprise, Stuyvesant consented to them. Usually the victor dictates the terms of a peace settlement, and up to this time Stuyvesant had insisted upon unconditional surrender. In this case the Swedes, who were being subdued, prepared the terms of surrender and naturally made them as lenient as possible, doubtless expecting Stuyvesant to expunge, or at least modify, some of the provisions. What caused Stuyvesant to display this leniency after all the threats he had made?

Stuyvesant must have realized that he was guilty of an error of judgement, because he had weakened the defenses at New Amsterdam in order to strengthen his forces for an attack on New Sweden. After his flotilla left, the Indians sought to avenge themselves against Dutch abuse and mistreatment, which had reached its climax in the merciless slaughter of Indian families during Governor Kieft's administration. A fleet of sixty-four canoes carrying at least 500 Indian warriors made a surprise landing at New Amsterdam; Indians began to run riot through the town. In the evening they were joined by an additional 200 warriors. The Dutch burgher corps went to the defense of the residents, and the Indians crossed the river and began a three-day orgy of murder, arson, and robbery. Staten Island and the settlement of Pavonia were completely laid waste. At least fifty colonists were murdered in cold blood; a hundred more, mostly women and children, were carried away as captives; and 200 others, who escaped death and capture, lost their properties and possessions. Twenty-eight boweries and thousands of bushels of grain recently harvested went up in smoke; 500 or 600 head of cattle were either slaughtered or stolen.

The day Rising handed his proposed peace terms to Stuyvesant, the latter had received a letter, carried by a friendly Indian runner, from members of his council who remained to govern New Amsterdam, reporting the details of the uprising. The council urged Stuyvesant to return home at once to save the colony from further destruction. Stuyvesant's own family was in grave danger, the council having hired ten Frenchmen to protect his wife and children and the plantation where they lived. In a second letter appended to the first, members of the council recommended that Stuyvesant should "arrange as soon as possible, some provisional contract with the [Swedish] governor concerning the fort and the lands of Cristina, with the most favorable conditions possible for this country and which honor allows; and to return here at the first opportunity with the ships and men in order to preserve what is still left."

Stuyvesant read the tragic news shortly before conferring with Rising, but to disclose it would weaken his bargaining position. Rising knew nothing about the Indian attack nor that Stuyvesant had received a message telling him of the crucial need for his soldiers in New Amsterdam. If Rising had built up his strength at Fort Christina instead of at Fort Casimir would he have been less willing to surrender so early? There is little question that Stuyvesant would have been able to take the fort in time with his superior forces, but could he have afforded to delay his return to New Amsterdam by prolonging the action against the Swedes? As it turned out, Stuyvesant's only recourse was to accept the peace terms no matter how much they seemed to appease the Swedes. Both he and Rising signed the document on September 15, and Rising still did not know why Stuyvesant had accepted the terms in such haste. Stuyvesant even allowed the Swedish officers held captive at Fort Casimir to be released and come to Fort Christina for the signing.

One of the provisions in the peace treaty allowed Rising, Van Elswick, and the other officers and soldiers, as well as the freemen, the choice of remaining as Dutch subjects or returning to Sweden at Dutch expense. Stuyvesant agreed to provide ships to transport them and their movable property to New Amsterdam and from there to Holland and thence to Gothenburg. Swedes or Finns who elected to remain in the colony would be permitted to pursue their livelihood "as good and free inhabitants," with the privilege of observing Lutheranism under the Augsburg Confession and to have their own religious instructors.

Both Rising and Van Elswick wanted the record to show that they had not been vanquished in ignominious defeat, and the treaty provided for the Swedish soldiers to march out of the fort and occupy shelters on Timber Island "with drums beating, pipes playing, flags flying, slow-matches burning, musketballs in their mouths, carrying hand and side arms. . . ." This symbolized an honorable and voluntary surrender without loss of face.

As soon as Fort Christina was vacated, Stuyvesant and his

STUYVESANT'S FLEET ATTACKS FORT TREFALDIGHET (TRINITY)
AND SWEDEN SURRENDERS THE FORT.

NEXT HE LAYS SIEGE TO FORT CHRISTINA AND SWEDEN
SURRENDERS THE FORT AND ALL OF NEW
SWEDEN FALLS TO THE DUTCH ON
SEPTEMBER 15, 1655.

STUYVESANT'S TENT
WHERE SURRENDER
TERMS WERE SIGNED

officers entered the fort. Stuyvesant invited Rising to join him for another conference. During this discussion Rising learned for the first time of the Indian massacre and why Stuyvesant had been so willing to accept the Swedish peace terms. It was also apparent why Stuyvesant was in a hurry to dismantle the batteries, withdraw his troops, and return to New Amsterdam. Then Stuyvesant made an unusual proposition. He offered to give Fort Christina back to the Swedes on the condition that they would harbor no ill feelings toward the Dutch and that they would make an offensive and defensive alliance with each other. Rising was nonplussed by this unexpected offer and said he would have to confer with his officers about it.

Stuyvesant did not explain why he made this seemingly generous offer, but the reason is obvious. He did not offer to return Fort Casimir, because he had already decided he could hold it by leaving a small Dutch garrison there when he sailed away. However, holding Fort Christina secure against a possible Swedish coup to recover what they had lost would require a larger occupation force than he could spare in view of the crisis on the Hudson; his instructions also allowed him this option.

Rising and his officers discussed Stuyvesant's offer. They could not reconcile it with his earlier threats of unconditional surrender, and they were suspicious of his sincerity. They could not guarantee that the settlers of New Sweden would accept the Dutch as friends in view of the way their farms and houses had been pillaged.

Furthermore, Rising and his officers believed that their acceptance of Stuyvesant's terms might negate the claims they expected the Swedish government to make against the Dutch for indemnities resulting from damage done to the colony during the unprovoked assault. They also believed they could not subsist in New Sweden during the approaching winter because their food supply had been depleted and their cattle mostly slaughtered by Dutch soldiers. Many farms were ruined, and there were no trade goods in the storehouse to be used to barter with the Indians or to buy their friendship. They unanimously decided to reject Stuyvesant's offer and resign themselves to

God's mercy and the benevolence of the Swedish government to redress the wrongs Stuyvesant had inflicted upon them. By reading between the lines one gathers an impression that many of those who had come with Rising, including Rising himself, were not unhappy to leave New Sweden and return to the civilized country from whence they came. Who can blame them?

In the time that remained before Stuyvesant left the Delaware, Rising prepared a written inventory of all the assets in the colony that belonged to the Crown of Sweden—fortifications, houses, buildings, estates and farms, guns, ammunition, the remaining cattle, horses, oxen and swine, and everything else of importance. The inventory was signed and sealed by both Rising and Stuyvesant as evidence of what was temporarily retained in Stuyvesant's possession. The Swedish and Dutch governments would eventually have to decide what reparations, if any, would have to be made that would be mutually acceptable.

One final item of business remained to be conducted, an examination of Captain Sven Skute's conduct in surrendering Fort Casimir to Stuyvesant. Rising had included that condition in the peace terms that Stuyvesant signed, clearly emphasizing his concern about Skute's loyalty. The hearing or inquest was held on Timber Island, possibly at Rising's residence. Testimony offered by some of the officers and soldiers was damaging to Skute. In his own defense, supported by some of the other officers and men, Skute claimed that the soldiers were mutinous and when he ordered them to fight they refused. In fact, one of the Swedish soldiers was shot through the leg by Lieutenant Gyllengren as he tried to desert by climbing over the wall. He later died from the wound, the only known casualty in Stuyvesant's invasion: one Swedish soldier killed by his own officer. The evidence brought out in the hearing was inconclusive, and Rising made no decision for or against Skute. Skute himself sent a copy of the inquest and a letter in his own defense to Chancellor Eric Oxenstierna in Stockholm, but it is not known what action, if any, was taken. Skute never pled his case in Sweden, because he decided to remain on the Delaware as a freeman under the Stuyvesant government. Lieutenant Elias Gyllengren also decided to remain with him.

Ultimately thirty-seven males, including some soldiers, several freemen, Hendrick Van Elswick, Lieutenant Höök, Peter Lindeström, and the two pastors, Matthias Nertunius and Peter Hiört, left the colony to return home. Wives and children also accompanied them, but the exact number of family dependents who returned to Sweden is not known. Two boys, sons of Armegot and Papegoja, returned without their mother, who remained in the colony. Pastor Lock (Laurentius Carolus Lockenius) also remained behind, then the only remaining Lutheran pastor on the Delaware. The departing Swedes and Finns left the colony on October 11, 1655. After a sojourn in New Amsterdam, Stuyvesant assigned them to three different vessels with their baggage, and on October 23 they went to sea.

New Sweden as a political entity ended with the signing of peace terms between Stuyvesant and Rising on September 15, 1655. The story of New Sweden did not have a happy ending, but by no means did the political defeat mean the downfall of Swedish culture and religion. The number of men, women, and children who remained in the former New Sweden territory after Rising's departure is not known, but the total population was doubtless less than 250 or 300. The names of nineteen males are listed as signers of an oath pledging allegiance to Governor Stuyvesant, the government of the United Netherlands, and the directors of the West India Company. They promised not to engage in any hostile act but to conduct themselves as obedient and faithful subjects as long as they lived "at the South River of New Netherland."

Their names are given below as recorded in the document, but the reader should be aware that the same names may appear in other documents under different spellings. Only five signed their names; these are shown by asterisks; the others, who were illiterate, made their marks.

Jan Eckhoff*
Constantinus Gronenbergk*
Thoomas Bruyn
William Morris*
Harman Janse
Anies Gostoffson*
Baernt Jansen
Oloff Fransen
Andries Jansen
Jan Justen
Jan Schoffel
Marten Martense
Klaes Tomasse
Lambert Michelse
Mathys Esselse
Timen Stiddem*
Samuel Peterse
Lucas Petersen
Moens Andriesen

Other Swedes and Finns may have signed the same oath, but this one undated document seems to be the only survivor. Exactly where the above signatories were then residing is not stated. Most of them probably lived in the environs of Fort Casimir, because the Swedes and Finns occupying houses there were not dispossessed during Stuyvesant's invasion; others may have lived near Fort Christina; and still others in the Chester-Marcus Hook area and at Tinicum Island, Kingsessing, Aronameck, Passayunk, and elsewhere.

Since there was no longer a Swedish governor and council to represent the Swedish government, the Dutch now held the political reins. Before leaving for New Amsterdam, Stuyvesant assigned Captain Dirck Smith (sometimes spelled Smit or Smidt) as the provisional commander of New Sweden with his head-quarters at Fort Casimir. Smith commanded a company of sixty soldiers during the invasion. Some of those soldiers remained to garrison the fort, but the majority returned with Stuyvesant to assist in the defense of New Netherland against the Indians. Since Smith seemed to have little fear that the Swedes would rebel after Rising and his officers left the Delaware, he assigned only three or four soldiers to Fort Christina. Although the directors of the West India Company had a low esteem for the fort because of its location, they wanted to keep it in Dutch possession. Stuyvesant had already made a strong case that Fort Casimir was the best military position to control the Delaware and that it potentially held the greatest promise for a Dutch town. History proved that Stuyvesant was right—at least for the duration of the colonial period. New Castle became a cosmopolitan town before the city of Wilmington came into existence and before Philadelphia was laid out. The Swedes and Finns played an important part in the growth of the town, even after the fall of New Sweden, but that is another chapter in the history of the Delaware valley that goes well beyond the present account on which the curtain fell in 1655.

The reader is probably curious about what happened to the two leading adversaries, Governor Stuyvesant and Director Rising. Stuyvesant returned to New Amsterdam in time to protect the New Netherland from destruction, but the colony continued to face Indian troubles for many years with sporadic assaults and temporary peace settlements. Eventually the coastal Algonkian peoples were subjugated or gave up the futile goal of trying to repel the European invaders, whose numbers increased as the Indian population decreased from the toll taken by wars, alcoholism, small pox, and other diseases. By 1664, New Netherland attained a population of close to 10,000 people, of whom 1,500 resided in New Amsterdam. That year James, Duke of York, launched an attack against the New Netherland with an overpowering naval force. Stuyvesant was forced to surrender due to inadequate defenses, and on September 8, 1664, New Amsterdam became New York. With the English in control, Stuyvesant retired to his bowerie on Manhattan Island where he spent his last years. He died there a crotchety old man, still respected, and known to everyone as "the General."

Johan Rising returned safely to Sweden, although he did not receive a hero's welcome and never lived down the blame for the loss of the colony. He was given the position as general inspector over the collection of tolls in Prussia and Pomerania, an assignment unbefitting his abilities, and one he did not enjoy. He left office and was long without employment, becoming a victim of financial reverses. He claimed he was never paid all the salary due him for his services in New Sweden, and this made him bitter against the government. His ambition in his later years was to complete an important economic work entitled *A Treatise on Commerce*. Barely able to pay his rent or buy food and clothing, he worked under great difficulty. Although he never finished what would have been a monumental work, he completed a number of shorter economic treatises, a book on agriculture, and a journal and relations pertaining to New Sweden. He died in a miserable hovel, deeply in debt, a victim of extreme hardship and privation.

Coincidentally, Stuyvesant and Rising died the same year—1672. Stuyvesant's administration of New Netherland covered a seventeen-year period in contrast to the brief one year and four months that Rising spent in New Sweden. In one sense of the word they both failed, but they both faithfully performed as dedicated stewards and deserve their place in history. Their shortcomings, if there were any, were not due to weakness of character or disposition but due largely to circumstances beyond their control.

9. AFTERMATH

While Stuyvesant was consolidating his forces to besiege Fort Christina after having seized Fort Trinity, plans were being crystallized across the sea in Sweden to send supplies and new settlers to Rising on the ship *Mercurius*. Neither the officers of the South (New Sweden) Company, which had undergone another reorganization, nor the Commercial College were yet aware that Stuyvesant had invaded New Sweden. If they had known, it would have disrupted their plans, but they went ahead, after numerous delays at Gothenburg, to make the vessel ready by hiring a crew, purchasing and loading supplies, and selecting passengers in conformity with the new Swedish policy of permitting only respectable, law-abiding persons to go to New Sweden. At last, on November 25, 1655, the *Mercurius* sailed out to sea. This was more than two months after Rising had surrendered the colony to Stuyvesant, but the bad news had not yet reached Sweden.

Johan Papegoja and Hendrick Huygen were co-commanders of the expedition, Papegoja in charge of the people, and Huygen engaged to serve as the commissary in New Sweden in command of the vessel. The reader will recall that both men had served several tours of duty in the colony and that Papegoja was temporarily in command before Rising arrived and seized Fort Casimir. Papegoja returned home after Rising's arrival and a year later was on his way back to New Sweden.

The urgency of passengers to board the *Örn* when she left for the colony on February 2, 1654, was repeated as the *Mercurius* was being prepared for the voyage. There were more passengers than could be accommodated. The majority came from northern Sweden, where there were many Finns. Some were in such a hurry to get to Gothenburg before the vessel sailed that they sold their houses and belongings for much less than they were worth. Many of the families were rejected because of limited space aboard ship, a rejection that Papegoja wrote caused much "lamentation and weeping." The urge to leave for the New World may have reflected the struggle of the peasants against a deteriorating economy that had developed in Sweden. There may also have been political motivations. It would be interesting to know how many would have been fixed on leaving their homes if they had known that on their arrival in New Sweden they would be required to take an oath of allegiance to the Dutch.

Huygen made the following list of those who were given passage.

Officers and old servants	9
Swedish women	2
Swedish maidens	2
Finnish men, old and young	33
Finnish women	16
Finnish maidens	11
Finnish children aged 12 and younger	32
	105

Apparently a few additional names were added, possibly including those who wanted to rejoin members of their families in the colony. Those additions may have increased the passenger list to 110, and with twenty crew members, the total complement of "souls" aboard the *Mercurius* was about 130.

After a four-month voyage, the vessel arrived in the Delaware River on March 14, 1656. Papegoja must have been stunned at what he saw. The Swedish flag was no longer flying at Fort Trinity or over Fort Christina, where he and Armegot and their children had lived before he left for Sweden. Dutch colors were now waving in the wind at both forts. With the colony in Dutch hands how could he discharge the passengers "at or near Fort Christina," as he was instructed? Huygen was no less disquieted to find the West India Company in full control because he faced the possibility that his cargo might be confiscated if the vessel landed.

The two commanders were particularly disturbed that the Dutch would not allow the *Mercurius* to sail upriver to Tinicum Island, which had become the center of Swedish-Finnish activity following Rising's capitulation. With Christinahamn destroyed by fire and other farms pillaged, many of the Scandinavian families moved north of the Christina River. Dirck Smith, the provisional commander at Fort Casimir, had been replaced by a "Vice Director and Chief Magistrate" named Jean Paul Jacquet, recently arrived from Holland as a West India Company employee subordinate to Governor Stuyvesant. Some Scandinavians were then living in the vicinity of Fort Casimir, which was beginning to appear as a small-scale cosmopolitan community, but they were helpless to befriend the passengers on the *Mercurius*. Stuyvesant had earlier instructed Jacquet to keep a watchful eye on the Swedes, allowing none to remain in the fort overnight where they might foment trouble. If Jacquet found any Swedish residents of the Santhoeck antagonistic to the Dutch, he was further instructed to make them leave "with all possible politeness."

Prior to the arrival of the *Mercurius*, Jacquet reported to Stuyvesant that it was rumored some of the Swedes were inciting the Indians to turn against the townsfolk. Stuyvesant instructed him to insist that all of the Swedes who had not already signed the oath of allegiance should be required to do so. Those who refused to sign, or who contravened their oaths, should be sent away. Jacquet was naturally suspicious at the unexpected arrival of a Swedish ship with ten cannon visible in her gunports and under the command of men recognized as Swedish officers who had long opposed the Dutch. Furthermore, one of the commanders was known to be the son-in-law of Printz, the former militant governor, and it was learned that the adult male passengers aboard the vessel outnumbered the soldiers in the Dutch garrison. How could Jacquet be sure the *Mercurius* was not a Trojan horse traveling to the colony on the wings of the wind with military activists disguised as Finnish peasants? Jacquet was suspicious when Huygen came ashore to confer with him, so he arrested him as a traitor and an enemy of the state and then immediately sent a courier to Stuyvesant for further instructions.

When Stuyvesant received Jacquet's message he called an emergency session of the council, where it was decided the *Mercurius* must not be allowed to land the passengers. Instructions were returned to Jacquet that he should order the Swedish officers to bring the *Mercurius* to New Amsterdam, where provisions would be supplied for the vessel's return to Sweden. Both Papegoja and Huygen objected, and Jacquet agreed to allow Huygen to go overland to New Amsterdam for further discussion with Stuyvesant. Papegoja probably remained aboard the *Mercurius* at anchor opposite Fort Casimir during Huygen's absence.

Huygen subsequently appeared before Stuyvesant and his council, presenting a written petition that asked that the passengers be permitted to settle on the Delaware. Huygen pledged he would try to maintain friendly relations between the Swedes and the Dutch and would also assist in preventing Indian disturbances. Huygen's ability to converse in the Lenape dialect, and the friendship he had developed in the past with the leading chiefs, was well known to the Dutch. Huygen also requested the council to show compassion to the innocent passengers aboard the *Mercurius* who had been confined in overcrowded quarters ever since the vessel left Sweden and were anxious to debark. He said that "parents are separated from their children, even the husband from his wife." That was not an exaggeration because he knew that Papegoja's wife, Armegot, and those of her children who were then living in Printzhoff, had been separated from him for more than a year.

The council read Huygen's petition, but they politely denied his request. They told him that if the *Mercurius* did not come to New Amsterdam as ordered, they would send the warship *Wagh* "to bring or drive away the Swedish ship." This left Huygen no other option than to send a message to Papegoja urging him to bring the *Mercurius* and her passengers to New Amsterdam. He would remain in New Amsterdam and await their arrival so that he could return to Sweden with the vessel.

What happened when Papegoja received the message is not known, but he did not reply, nor did Stuyvesant receive satisfactory information from Jacquet at Fort Casimir. After an impatient wait Stuyvesant dispatched a squad of soldiers overland to learn what was going on and what was the cause of the delay. A week later he was informed that while Papegoja was preparing to comply with his instructions to leave the Delaware, a large party of Lenape warriors surrounded the Swedish ship in their canoes and some climbed aboard. They knew that the vessel had trade goods in her cargo (which Rising promised would be sent to them), and they insisted that the Swedes remain to trade with them. If Papegoja refused, they threatened to exterminate all the Swedes and Dutch living in the Delaware valley. Some of the Swedish freemen, apprehensive of the possible loss of their properties and the death of loved ones, sent a message to Papegoja imploring him not to sail away and leave them to the mercy of angry savages. Papegoja was left with only one course of action to protect *both* Swedes and Dutch; he ordered the skipper of the *Mercurius* to proceed up the river to Tinicum Island, where the frightened passengers disembarked. Some of the members of Stuyvesant's council who listened to the report believed that the whole episode was a contrived crisis staged by Swedes and Indians acting in cooperation to deceive the Dutch. But there was no evidence to prove that and Stuyvesant's inquiries convinced him that the incident was not planned by the skipper or the ship's crew, which meant the governor had no basis for taking punitive action because it was impossible for Papegoja to obey his orders.

By the time Stuyvesant's troops arrived on the Delaware the debarkation was an accomplished fact. Supplies had apparently been safely landed and hidden. The men, women, and children had dispersed, some swallowed up in the woods, where they probably built temporary kotas, and others sharing cabins with friends or relatives. The Dutch did not have a list of the names of the passengers and their ages, and little could be gained by trying to track them down since it was apparent they were mostly harmless farm families intending no injury to the Dutch.

Having landed the passengers, the crew took the *Mercurius* to Amsterdam as ordered, and Stuyvesant permitted the vessel to return to Sweden. Neither Huygen nor Papegoja were aboard when she weighed anchor. Papegoja, after visiting his family, returned to Sweden on another vessel. As previously mentioned, he and Armegot had an unhappy marriage, and this was another occasion of separation. Huygen gave Stuyvesant his bond to behave as a friendly visitor and was allowed to return to the Delaware with the understanding that he would do his best to influence the Lenape to remain peaceful. The approximate 110 harmless "souls" melded into the Scandinavian population as permanent settlers, subject to the Dutch government. Years later their descendants would tell of their safe, but belated arrival, on the *Mercurius* on the twelfth and last official Swedish expedition to America—after Sweden had been overthrown by the Dutch.

From 1655 to 1664 the Dutch ruled the territory formerly known as New Sweden, first as a possession of the West India Company under the direction of Peter Stuyvesant, and later as a colony governed by the city of Amsterdam in Holland. It was a complicated situation, and there were both political and geographical changes that are important to the historian but would require more detail to explain than space permits. The important thing for the reader to know is that during Stuyvesant's administration of the New Netherland, he continued to maintain his headquarters on Manhattan Island, and he appointed the top officials in the Delaware colony. However, he and his council retained the right to make major decisions within the framework of the policies of the West India Company. Subsequently, when the city of Amsterdam took over control of the colony from the West India Company, the burgomasters of the city appointed a director for the colony. The city in effect ruled the colony and paid its own soldiers to protect the colonists sent from Holland, some in the city's employ. The town at the former Fort Casimir was given a new name, New Amstel, and it became the center of the political and economic life in the Delaware colony.

There were Swedish families living in New Amstel when the city of Amsterdam acquired the colony, and a small Swedish-Finnish settlement was subsequently made at the "Second Hook" north of the town in the vicinity of present Swanwyck. A few of the Swedes living at New Amstel were formerly Rising's military officers, such as Elias Gyllengren and Sven Skute, who had become civilians. Two or three former Swedish soldiers served as members of the Dutch garrison, and Timen Stiddem, the Swedish barber-surgeon, practiced medicine for a time in the Dutch town.

Most of the Swedes were not disposed to live in towns, preferring small farms with marshes and navigable creeks separating their lands from their neighbor's. Some settled in the vicinity of Fort Christina, which the Dutch renamed Fort Altena, and others cultivated the fertile fields in the area lying between the Brandywine and Christina, which many years later comprised lots within the city of Wilmington. The Swedish and Finnish population in the New Amstel-Fort Altena environs was not static, and some residents like Dr. Stiddem and Jan Stalcop, for example, moved from New Amstel to new plantations now embraced within the bounds of Wilmington; others like Sven Skute and Gregorius van Dyck moved upriver to lands as far north as the Schuylkill River, where other Swedes had settled. That mobility can partly be explained by their desire to live among people of their own nation, as opposed to associating with non-Swedes in a government under the control of Dutch officials. The Dutch language may also have been a barrier to some families. The Finns actually spoke a language among themselves that differed from Swedish, but most could now speak and understand Swedish.

There was also the matter of church attendance, an important consideration for devout Lutherans who had no church at New Amstel where they could be married, have their babies baptized, or attend a high mass where communion was served. The influence of the little church on Tinicum Island in bringing the families together should not be underestimated. There was still a small chapel at Fort Altena, but there was no pastor. Pastor Lock, then the only Swedish minister left on the Delaware, preached at Tinicum and only infrequently came down the river to visit Lutheran families. Nevertheless, they evidently felt the need to attend services regularly and to celebrate the religious holidays in the Tinicum church where there was a resident pastor.

Another important factor contributed to the consolidation of the Scandinavian families in the territory readily accessible to Tinicum Island. Governor Stuyvesant reached the conclusion that it was to the best interests of the Dutch to allow the Swedes limited local autonomy in handling their own judicial and political affairs. An entry in the records of New Amstel dated August 14, 1656—less than a year after Rising's surrender— discloses the surprising information that Vice-Director Jacquet notified Gregorius van Dyck that Stuyvesant had named him the first "deputy schout among the Swedish nation" and that he had also appointed Swedish magistrates to preside at their own court seated on Tinicum Island. Van Dyck, a native of the Hague, was a Swedish subject by choice; he served as an officer under Ridder, Printz, and Rising and was unswerving in his loyalty to Swedish interests. Stuyvesant also granted the residents of the former New Sweden a right they had not previously enjoyed; he made land grants to individual citizens and confirmed ownership to them by patents for houses and plantations. Land grants were not confined to freemen; Stuyvesant made grants to soldiers and servants who wanted to own their own property. As legal property owners with a voice in their local government and having their own magistrates, the Swedes and Finns became members of an enclave on the Delaware with a political identity separate from the Dutch at Fort Casimir or Fort Altena. The upriver Scandinavians were frequently referred to as "the Swedish nation."

The new magistrates sat as a court on Tinicum Island as early as 1657, although their adoptive system of jurisprudence differed in form from the dictatorial courts Printz and Rising had previously held. The new system was modelled after the Dutch court at New Amstel. The court tried civil and criminal cases within certain prescribed limits. It also had regulatory functions such as arbitrating disputes over debts, disciplining unruly residents, recording marital engagements, building dikes and bridges, improving roads, etc. Although the deputy schout was the chief executive officer, combining the role of sheriff and prosecuting attorney, unlike an English sheriff, he was an ex-officio member of the court that sat as a group, deliberated in private, and then rendered its decision. Stuyvesant and his council sat as an appeal court for the litigants, if an appeal was necessary.

On an inspection trip to the Delaware in May of 1658, Stuyvesant visited the court on Tinicum Island, which was then composed of Deputy Schout van Dyck and the magistrates Peter Cock, Mats Hansson, Peter Gunnarsson Rambo, and Olof Stille. During the visit Stuyvesant approved the Swedes' request that they be allowed to form their own militia company with three officers, Sven Skute, captain, Anders Dalbo, lieutenant, and Jacob Swensson, ensign. Those officers were not strangers to Stuyvesant—they were all on duty at Fort Trinity when he attacked New Sweden three years before, but he showed no rancor and approved their selection. Were they not now Dutch subjects owing their loyalty to him?

The magistrates requested that they be given proper instructions to enable them to perform the duties entrusted them, which is an admission that they were not familiar with Dutch legal procedures. They also requested, and were given permission, to engage a court messenger to summon litigants in the community, where the residents were widely scattered, and to run official errands for the court. The magistrates also requested that they have open lines of communication for ready access to Willem Beeckman, the Dutch commissary and vice-director at Fort Altena, a Stuyvesant appointee, so that in a serious emergency Dutch troops could be sent to their assistance.

Next to nothing is known about the cases tried by the magistrates, and it is uncertain where they convened since there is no record of a courthouse on Tinicum Island. The magistrates must have met at designated times, perhaps quarterly, and remained in session until their business was completed. Then they returned to their farms or trades to pursue a living. They received no fixed salaries or expenses; whatever small compensation was paid them must have been derived from fines and certain fees.

When the directors of the West India Company learned in Holland that Stuyvesant delegated authority to the Swedes in their own magistrates court and permitted them to have militia officers, they were disturbed and displeased. They wrote that they did not believe the Swedes should be allowed to have their own court and that Dutchmen should be appointed as the terms of the Swedes expired. The directors also strongly opposed allowing the Swedes to have their own militia officers and, under the misapprehension that Stuyvesant intended to supply the Swedish militia with weapons, protested that "they will know well how to use against us."

Stuyvesant replied that he knew the Swedes did not have a great affection for the Dutch, but in his judgment the best method for handling them was to show leniency and "to win their hearts and divert their thoughts from a hard and tyrannical form of government." Nevertheless, he added he would observe the director's wishes "as far as possible agreeable to circumstances and occasion." The directors may have had some reason for their apprehension, because as of March 1660 van Dyck reported that the "Swedish and Finnish nation number about 130 men capable of bearing arms." There were not that many Dutch soldiers at Fort Altena and Fort Casimir combined. Van

Dyck was undoubtedly referring only to the able-bodied males living north of Fort Altena, where the population must have been steadily increasing. Six years before when Rising surrendered, a Dutch minister accompanying Stuyvesant estimated that there were "at least 200 Swedes and Finns" in the area *north of Fort Christina*, and he was speaking of the total population. With the arrival of *Mercurius,* additional "souls" increased the population, but it is uncertain how many lived south of Fort Altena. In the absence of an official census, estimates can only be conjectural, but the Scandinavian population in the entire Delaware valley in 1660 probably did not exceed more than 400 or 500 men, women, amd children.

In 1661, Stuyvesant dismissed Gregorius van Dyck as deputy schout and appointed a Dutchman, Willem Beeckman, as the chief justice of the court, which would have pleased the directors. However, Peter Cock, Mats Hanson, and Olof Stille were still in office as magistrates when Beeckman summoned the court into session several times at Fort Altena. The main seat continued to be on Tinicum Island, and although it was an inconvenient location for him, Beeckman also met there with the magistrates. His relations with the Swedes were friendly, and he did his best when the situation demanded to be conciliatory. The chief thing in opposition to him was that he was Dutch!

On March 12, 1664, Charles II of England granted his brother James Stuart, Duke of York (later to become James II) a patent that included practically all of the New Netherland. Parliament and the king agreed that the land in America claimed by Holland should be taken because it belonged to England by right of prior discovery. That move was part of an imperious plan to secure England's economic position in the New World. The grant to the Duke of York was the direct result of the effort to create a self-sufficient British empire from which foreign trade and commerce would be excluded. With the king's consent and financial support, the duke sent a naval squadron to America composed of warships, sailors, and 400 or 450 soldiers to seize the New Netherland.

As mentioned in the previous chapter, Stuyvesant was forced to surrender Fort Amsterdam and Manhattan Island to the Duke of York's warships and troops, giving the English control of the heart of New Netherland. The duke's instructions to his officials said nothing about New Amstel, which actually was not included in his grant, but it was immediately apparent to his officials that the mission would not be accomplished unless the territory on the west side of the Delaware governed by the city of Amsterdam were taken.

The city's colony now extended "from the sea upwards as far as the river reaches," and included a small Mennonite settlement at Lewes, the town of New Amstel, Fort Altena and the land that later became the city of Wilmington, and all the upriver territory along the Delaware occupied by Swedes and Finns, including Tinicum Island and the Schuylkill drainage system. The director of the city's colony was a former Dutch army officer named Alexander d'Hinoyossa, who had developed a profitable business for the colony by trading with merchants in Maryland and shipping tobacco, lumber, furs, and grains to Holland. D'Hinoyossa imported additional Swedish and Finnish farmers to reinforce the population, and he encouraged his Scandinavian subjects to raise surplus grains and other products that could be exported. As of 1664, the Swedes and Finns had 110 farms, 2,000 cows and oxen, 20 horses, 80 sheep, and several thousand swine. Many of the freemen were more prosperous than they had ever been.

The Duke of York's officers were determined to halt the Dutch commercial expansion and to take over that business for England's benefit. On October 1, 1664, English warships appeared in the Delaware River and a few days later landed an invasion force at New Amstel. Although there were less than fifty Dutch soldiers in the garrison at the fort, d'Hinoyossa ordered them to resist the invaders. The English troops, well equipped and in superior numbers, overran the fort and the town, confiscating merchandise, livestock, tools, cannon, ammunition, black slaves intended to be traded in Maryland, and everything else belonging to the city of Amsterdam, as well as the houses and lands owned by Director d'Hinoyossa and other officials. New Amstel, which was then named New Castle by the English, and all of the city's colony on the Delaware became the Duke of York's property.

The Duke of York's troops did not molest any of the Swedish and Finnish families on the river. There was no need for them to do so—the Swedes offered no resistance or objections to the English assault. They never fully resigned themselves to a Dutch administration and they had not forgotten the pillage of their homes and farms in Stuyvesant's invasion of New Sweden in 1655.

The English offered very generous surrender terms. Everyone who consented to accept the authority of the English government, Dutch, Swedes, Finns, and all others, were permitted to remain and enjoy all the rights of Englishmen. As such they would be protected by English law and justice with permission to own real and personal property and to "enjoy the liberty of their Conscience in Church Discipline as formerly." The Duke of York's government later confirmed the land patents that the Dutch had issued to them, and those settlers who did not have a legal claim to their lands were issued new patents.

The incumbent magistrates, both Dutch and Swedes, became subordinate to the Duke of York's commander, but they were permitted to continue in office and wield their authority as before. The schouts, burgomasters, and inferior magistrates were allowed to exercise their customary authority within their own precincts for a period of six months, or until further administrative changes were agreed upon. The political processes and the administration of justice remained more Dutch than English. Anyone who did not want to stay in the colony under English rule was free to depart with his possessions within a six-month period. There was no reason for any Swedes or Finns to leave. Nothing was taken away from them, and they retained the right to hold their own magistrates court, attend their own churches, and live as they had done under the Dutch government. The difference was that they were now English subjects obliged to obey the Duke of York's laws. But the magistrates knew nothing about the content of the duke's laws!

The duke's laws became effective in written form in New York City, Long Island, Staten Island, and Westchester in 1665, but they were not extended to the Delaware colony until 1676. The eleven-year hiatus gave everyone ample time for adjustment to the new regime and for an influx of English residents that resulted in an increase of mixed marriages.

The Swedish magistrates court moved from Tinicum Island to Upland (present-day Chester), where it was seated when the Duke of York's laws became official on the Delaware. In the first written record of the Upland Court that has survived there is a transcript of a document filed in the session of November 14, 1676, that bears the signature of Edmund Andros, the governor appointed by the Duke of York to preside over "all his Territories in America." It reads in part as follows:

BY VIRTUE of the authority deryved unto me; I: doe hereby in his Majesties name, constitute appoint & authorize you Mr. Peter Cock, Mr. Peter Rambo, Mr. Israell Helm, Mr. Lace Andriesen, Mr. Oele Swen & Mr. Otto Ernest Cock to bee Justices of the Peace in the Jurisdiction of delowar river and dependencies and any three or more of you to bee a Court of Judicature . . .This Commission to bee of force for the space of one yeare after the date hereof, or till further order. Given under my hand and seale in New Yorke the 23rd day of September, in the 28th Yeare of his Majesties Raigne, Annoq Domini, 1676.

In the reorganization of the courts, Governor Andros also specified that two other courts be continued, one at New Castle and the other at the "Whorekill" (present-day Lewes). Andros also issued an important directive: thereafter, each court was required to keep an account of its proceedings written *in the English language*. In due time the Upland Court, originally composed of Scandinavian-Americans, evolved into the Court of Chester County, Pennsylvania, an outgrowth of the first magistrates court that convened on Tinicum Island, where Swedish was the accepted language.

Religious changes also occurred on the Delaware after the Duke of York took control of the Delaware colony. The Dutch magistrates at New Amstel long opposed the building of a Lutheran church in the town because they were prejudiced against any theology that did not conform to the Dutch Reformed church. In October of 1666, officials in New Amstel were informed that the duke approved of allowing the Lutherans to exercise their religious beliefs without disturbance. That helped pave the way for the Swedes to establish the Crane Hook Church on the south side of the Christina River in 1667. Readers who would like to have further information about that log church and its location should consult the book by Jeannette Eckman cited in the accompanying reading list.

The growth of the membership of the Crane Hook Church caused it to be vacated in 1699 in favor of a new and larger church built of stone on land where Fort Christina formerly stood. The fort had been demolished before this, having outlived its usefulness. Dedicated on June 4, 1699, the new church was known to the Swedes as Trefaldighets Kyrckia ("Holy Trinity Church"), now called "Old Swedes Church," the largest Swedish church on the Delaware when it was built. A book about the building of the church that also contains the records of the Swedish church prior to 1773, as translated by Horace Burr, is also found in the accompanying reading list.

When William Penn arrived in America in 1682 he acquired the territory owned by the Duke of York, which then became known as the "Three Lower Counties of Pennsylvania," namely, New Castle, Kent, and Sussex. The Swedes and Finns were affected in many ways by the new democratic government that Penn established and by the increase in population that followed. Penn required all existing property owners to surrender their former Dutch or English patents and have their lands resurveyed so that his government could issue new, more precisely worded patents, with accurate drawings of the properties.

That requirement, of course, applied to all the Swedish and Finnish property owners, whose lands became alienable. It also contributed to population shifts as Philadelphia became the capital of the Province of Pennsylvania and New Castle eventually became the second largest city in Penn's colony. The little log church on Tinicum Island was soon abandoned, and second-generation Swedes and Finns dispersed to other locations. "Chester," a visitor wrote at the time, "was once a small village of Swedes, although it is now overrun by English."

Members of the former Tinicum congregation, along with others, built a brick church in 1700 in Philadelphia called Gloria Dei, which tended to attract Swedish Lutherans to the area. Swedish and Finnish families who crossed the Delaware River to New Jersey founded the Raccoon Church in Gloucester County (present-day Swedesboro) and the Penn's Neck Church in Salem County (present-day Churchtown). Such Scandinavian names as Derickson, Mullica, Peterson, Justisson, and many others, were prominent on the church rolls, as were the names of Cock, Dalbo, Helm, Hendrickson, Lock, Mattson, Rambo, and others descended from members of the early parish on Tinicum Island. Probably some of the members could trace their paternity back to officers amd soldiers in New Jersey's first contingent of Swedes and Finns who occupied Fort Elfsborg in 1643. Prior to the building of those churches, land was patented to Swedes as early as 1668 in what is now Gloucester County, and some residents of New Jersey crossed the river to attend services at the Crane Hook Church as early as 1671.

It goes without saying that the Swedish presence in the Delaware River valley did not disappear when Rising surrendered New Sweden to the Dutch. In many ways the surrender was the beginning of an effective, self-perpetuating colonial society. The handful of Swedes that originally settled at Fort Christina slowly grew into a few hundred, but before the end of the Willian Penn period the fruitfulness of those immigrants grew into thousands of Swedish-Americans and Finnish-Americans. Many intermarried with peoples of other national backgrounds. Penn himself wrote that the Swedes had fine children and that it was "rare to find one of them without three or four boys, and as many girls." One of the Swedish immigrants who arrived on the second voyage of the *Kalmar Nyckel* in 1640 had thirty-seven grandchildren in America before his death. Another could boast of thirty-nine great-grandsons!

What elements in the Scandanavian folk culture diffused to other parts of young America as settlers pressed South and West? Reference has already been made to the first log cabins in America making their appearance in the Delaware valley. But what else can be pointed to as a Scandinavian influence in America? Can vestiges of Swedish culture be discerned in modern American life? What persons having Swedish and Finnish heritage played prominent roles in American political, economic, and artistic life? These and many other questions might be asked, but the answers go well beyond the scope of this little book. The story of New Sweden during the seventeen years it was in existence has been briefly told, but the sequel remains to be written after careful study by sociologists, anthropologists, social historians, geographers, and others.

One final question directly relating to New Sweden has not yet been answered: why did not the Swedish government take action to regain the colony from the Dutch? The answer is that attempts were made, starting in 1656 when the Swedish representative at the Hague demanded that the States General pay indemnity and restore the colony. The matter was referred to the West India Company at Amsterdam, where it was apparently tabled. Charles X of Sweden had serious intentions of regaining the colony either by diplomatic or military means, but wars with his neighbors required top priority, deferring further action.

In 1663, Swedish diplomats in Holland brought up the matter again, but the Dutch gave no indication of making restitution. However, they expressed concern about preparations being made in Sweden to commission two warships for a secret mission. On October 16, 1663, news reached Stuyvesant in New Amsterdam that one of the vessels was a frigate with thirty-two cannon and the other a yacht with eight or ten cannon. It was rumored that there were 200 or more soldiers aboard and that the vessels were getting ready to sail to America to recover New Sweden. Stuyvesant was ordered to be on his guard. Almost a year later Stuyvesant received a letter from the directors about "a wonderful work of the Lord worth noting and to be grateful for," because the Swedish expedition "had been delayed and prevented." On the way from Stockholm to Gothenburg the yacht was wrecked, and the frigate sailed alone, but its course was towards Africa, not the Delaware River.

Subsequently, many letters were written and diplomatic conferences held between Swedish and Dutch representatives, with discussion between the West India Company and the government of the Netherlands questioning whose responsibility it was. While that was going on, New Netherland fell to the Duke of York's troops and suddenly England owned the former New Sweden. Relations between Sweden and England were then friendly, but England could not be expected to turn over to Sweden the territory taken from the Dutch that the English claimed belonged to them and was illicitly seized by the Dutch in the first place. And why should the United Netherlands at that late date make restitution to Sweden for territory that now belonged to England? More meetings were held, letters written, and protests registered, but it was all useless and wasted energy. Neither Holland nor England paid any indemnity to Sweden, and no lands were restored. Sweden's colony in the New World was lost forever.

10. SIGHTS TO SEE

"I never saw a church like that before," my grandson said after we visited "Old Swedes" Church at 606 Church Street, where we had walked from Wilmington's Fort Christina Park.

"What do you mean?" I asked.

"There are dead people buried under the floor," he replied, "and it is paved with bricks."

"That was a Swedish custom a long time ago," I said. "Some of the early ministers and their children were buried in the church because it was considered a place to honor special people. Bricks were easier to remove for digging a grave than tearing up wood floors, and bricks never decayed like wood."

"Why do you have to open those little doors to get into the seats?" he asked.

"They are called box pews," I replied. "Each row of pews has its own door on the center aisle. In the old days the church was heated in the winter by a wood stove, and when the people took their seats they closed the little doors to protect their legs from cold drafts."

"The church is kind of like a museum," he said.

"There sure are a lot of interesting things to see," I answered, "like the black walnut pulpit, which they say is the oldest one in the United States. But don't forget it is a church, not a museum. It has about 100 members and services are held every Sunday. It used to be a Lutheran church and the services

were conducted in Swedish, but now it's a Protestant-Episcopal
church and everybody speaks English.''

After leaving the church we idled for a few minutes in the
churchyard looking at the inscriptions on the gravestones in the
shadows of several large sycamores. The hushed silence was
broken by the rumbling of an Amtrak locomotive slowing down
for the passenger stop at the Wilmington station. No one knows
how many graves were uprooted when the bed for the railroad
tracks was dug years ago. The earliest graves dated back to the
original Swedish and Finnish settlers living at and near Fort
Christina before the church was built and were marked with
field stones, some etched with the initials of the dead person.
After the church was constructed, the custom of using inscribed
gravestones was adopted, and although many are still legible,
the inscriptions on the oldest ones have weathered away.

Before leaving the churchyard we stopped to look at the
HENDRICKSON HOUSE on the church property, which is said
to have been built about 1690. It originally stood on Crum
Creek near Chester and was owned by a Swede named Andrew
Hendrickson, whose descendants lived in it until 1788 when it
was sold as a tenant farmhouse. It later was in danger of being
destroyed, so in 1958 it was moved to its present location for
use as a small history museum and office. Unlike the original
log dwellings built by the Swedes and Finns, it is a stone
dwelling with a shingled roof, the type of architecture a success-
ful Scandinavian farmer might adopt to replace a cabin built by
his father or grandfather. I was admiring how the stone house
had been skillfully reconstructed to preserve its original lines
when my young companion interrupted,

''Where are we going now?'' I gathered that if I wanted to
stimulate his interest in history that I had better speed up the
tour.

''I've already told you about the Swedish ship called the
Kalmar Nyckel,'' I said. ''How would you like to see where it
may be rebuilt?''

''What are they doing that for?'' he wanted to know. ''Did
the Indians set it on fire?''

I briefly explained as we walked to the KALMAR NYCKEL SHIPYARD on Seventh Street, a short distance east of Fort Christina Park, that the first *Kalmar Nyckel* ended its days in Sweden a long time ago after many years of service and that an organization called the Kalmar Nyckel Foundation was planning to duplicate the vessel. The objective is to rebuild a full-scale replica with sails, masts, spars, and other features as close to the original as possible. If the project materializes, the ship will be berthed at "the Rocks" where students, tourists, and other interested visitors can go aboard and step from the present back into the past and see a sailing vessel similar to the first *Kalmar Nyckel* that brought Swedish settlers to New Sweden on three different voyages, 1638, 1640, and 1641. Visitors can see the stocks on which the ship will be built and the old ways where it is expected to be launched if sufficient funds are raised.

My grandson and I then returned to our car and drove to the EAST SEVENTH STREET PARK at the far end of Seventh Street, a small grassy plot on the waterfront, a short distance above the junction of the Christina with the Delaware River, maintained as parkland by the city of Wilmington. A new dock has been built for the convenience of the visitor seeking a better view of the Christina.

"That's where Swedish ships like the *Kalmar Nyckel*, the *Fogel Grip*, the *Swan*, the *Eagle*, the *Golden Shark*, and others, sailed into the Minquas Kill from the Delaware," I said. "It was the last lap on the long dangerous voyage across the seas from Sweden to Fort Christina. When they rounded the curve in the stream and saw the Swedish flag waving over Fort Christina, it was like later generations seeing the Statue of Liberty—it meant the journey was over, and the people waiting at 'the Rocks' were thrilled to welcome them."

My sentiments seem to fall on deaf ears. "Look at all the big buildings you can see," he said, pointing in the opposite direction to Wilmington's ever-growing skyline in the west.

"The Swedes didn't have that kind of view from the river," I said. "There weren't any stores or office buildings when they arrived—just rivers, marshes, and woods. Things seem to have changed a lot, haven't they?''

He didn't answer, but he looked out at the Delaware River and then back again to the Wilmington skyline. I had a feeling that at that particular moment he was beginning to feel a sense of history for the first time.

"How would you like to take a ride down the Delaware River?''

My question came as a surprise to him. "In a ship like the ones the Swedes came in?'' he asked.

"No,'' I replied, "in my car, which is faster and much easier for me to handle. Some other time we will take a boat ride in the river.''

We drove back up Seventh Street, went left on Swedes Landing Road to the bridge over the Christina where Jean Paul Jacquet operated a ferry in the 1670s for the convenience of travelers between Fort Christina and New Castle. At the end of the bridge we turned south on Route 29, which Delawareans call "the river road'' because it parallels the Delaware. In about ten minutes we reached HISTORIC NEW CASTLE, where Peter Stuyvesant built Fort Casimir in 1651 and which the Swedes later seized and renamed Fort Trefaldighet.

The fort stood on the river front, east of where present Chestnut Street deadends at Second Street. Nothing remains of the fort today. Much of it was washed away or inundated by the river after it fell into disuse; the remaining surface debris was leveled off in 1678–79. The site is marked with a memorial sign erected by the state. Fortunately one can still enjoy a panoramic view of the "majestic Delaware,'' where in the distant past sailing craft from Sweden and Holland and coastal vessels from New Amsterdam, New England, and Virginia anchored at the long wooden pier to disembark their passengers or unload their cargoes. The pier, too, has long since disappeared.

The original residences in what were called the "First Row'' and the "Second Row,'' first occupied by Dutch and next by Swedish and Finnish families after Governor Johan Rising's conquest in 1654, have all been supplanted by more pretentious

HOLY TRINITY CHURCH

SKETCHED FROM AN EARLY DESCRIPTION OF THE CHURCH

"OLD SWEDES" CHURCH

BOX PEWS

COMMON TO 18TH CENTURY AMERICAN CHURCHES

HENDRICKSON HOUSE CIRCA 1690

"OLD SWEDES" IS THIS NATIONS OLDEST CHURCH STANDING AS ORIGINALLY BUILT AND IN USE TODAY.

FINNISH MEMORIAL TO THE DELAWARE COLONY OF NEW SWEDEN

WEST SIDE   EAST SIDE

PULPIT
OLDEST KNOWN PULPIT IN UNITED STATES MADE OF BLACK WALNUT, A NATIVE TREE IN DELAWARE

STONE MARKER
IT IS LOCATED AT THE APPROXIMATE SITE OF CRANE HOOK CHURCH. BUILT IN 1667

THE MEMORIAL IS IN A PARK IN CHESTER. THE FINNISH SCULPTURE WAS EXECUTED BY WÄINÖ AALTONEN IN 1938 FOR THE TRICENTENNIAL

THE MARKER IS LOCATED AT THE MARINE TERMINAL THE SICO OIL STORAGE PLANT. (HISTORICAL SOCIETY OF DELAWARE ERECTED IT IN 1896)

JOHN MORTONS GRAVE SIGNED THE DECLARATION OF INDEPENDENCE

EAST 7TH STREET PARK
AUTHOR AND YOUNG FRIEND

OLD SWEDES BURIAL GROUND - CHESTER, PA.

© N. SAWIN

homes built in the eighteenth and nineteenth centuries. The OLD DUTCH HOUSE, traditionally the town's oldest dwelling, is an exception, because it is believed to have been built between 1690 and 1701. The private homes, churches, and public buildings are enumerated in Jeannette Eckman's book cited in the reading list, and although they are not directly related to the Swedish occupancy, the interested visitor will enjoy seeing them. The cobbled street, brick sidewalks, and early architecture lend a colonial atmosphere to a leisurely walk through the Strand. My grandson was fascinated by the shining brass door knockers, the wooden shutters on the doors, as well as the windows. He was especially curious about the foot-scrapers on the marble door stoops and asked so many questions about so many things that I was certain that the history bug was beginning to bite!

After leaving New Castle, we turned off on Route 40 to the Delaware Memorial Bridge, which I told him was supposed to be one of the six largest suspension bridges in the world. We drove across the span towering over the river in about five minutes, in contrast to the laborious crossing made by the early Swedes when they paddled their dugout canoes from one side to the other. Before they had their own churches in New Jersey, those living at what were then called Raccoon and Penn's Neck often allowed two days to attend Sunday services at the churches at Crane Hook or Tinicum Island. They crossed the river on a Saturday and stayed overnight with friends or relatives to be on time for the early worship services on Sunday morning and a second service held in the afternoon. Regular evening services were unknown because of the difficulty of lighting the church after the sun went down and the difficulties of traveling in the dark. The three main religious celebrations: Christmas, Easter, and Pentecost, usually lasted about four days each, which caused inconveniences for those living on the east side of the river who attended church on the other side. That's why the Swedes who moved to New Jersey were so anxious to increase their population to justify building their own church.

At the east end of the bridge we bore south to Salem on

Route 49 where we crossed a small bridge over the old Varkens Kill, now called the Salem River. At the SALEM COUNTY HISTORICAL SOCIETY, 79-83 Market Street, we obtained directions for the short drive to Elsinboro Township on the Delaware River. A historical marker at the corner of Fort Elfsborg Road and Hancock Bridge Road states that Fort Elfsborg was built near there in 1643. However, the exact location of the fort still remains in doubt. Some believe it was south of Mill Creek, a tributary to the Delaware, and has been washed away; others conjecture that it was situated on an insular tract separated from the mainland by a narrow tidal stream and is now inundated by the river. The absence of contemporary drawings or detailed maps complicates the problem of verifying the location.

Joseph G. Lippincott, a Salem resident who has searched for the site of the fort since his boyhood, took us to a point of land immediately south of Anders Ditch and north Mill Creek where he has found the ends of unidentified log posts and an unusual deposition of flat stones visible only at low tide. His assumption is that the fort, now covered by the river waters, may have been at this point, and that possibility cannot be ruled out, although the evidence is still inconclusive.

"We didn't see a Swedish fort with its bastions overlooking the river," I said to my grandson as we left this low-lying tidal area, and returned to Route 49, "but I want to make this trip to New Jersey extra special for you. How would you like to visit some Lenape Indians?"

"Real Indians?" he asked in disbelief. "Didn't they all get killed?"

"Some were killed," I answered "and others died from small pox and other European diseases. Most of those who survived left the Delaware valley and moved west after their lands were sold. But a few members of the Lenape tribe did not want to leave. They kept their families alive by fishing and hunting and raising corn and vegetables in little gardens. Some of the Indian women made baskets and brooms which they sold to white settlers. As time went on, the families began to grow and there were marriages between Indian people and non-Indians. Because of their mixed blood these Indian descendants who were proud of being what they were kept to themselves, realizing that their ancestors were true "Native Americans."

"Do they still paint their faces and wear feathers in their hair?" he asked.

I tried to explain in words he could understand as we continued south to Bridgeton that the New Jersey Indian descendants live and dress like other people. They speak the English language and work in industry, the trades, and professions. Their children are enrolled in public and private schools, and the families attend Christian churches. Until recent years there was no bond to unite these people, but determined to preserve their native heritage, they formed an organization in 1978 called the Nanticoke-Lenni Lenape Indians of New Jersey, Inc. They have regular meetings and have their own elected officers, including a chief who bears the title of tribal chairman. The several hundred members of the organization live mostly in Cumberland, Salem, and Gloucester counties, the same area where the Lenape welcomed the Swedes during the administrations of Peter Hollander Ridder and Governor Johan Printz. It was then that they first began to sell their lands in southern New Jersey to the white men. Members of the present tribe hold a weekend powwow every fall, and they change their civilian clothing for Indian dress to socialize and perform Indian dances. Indian guests from other tribes also attend and participate, and thousands of non-Indian spectators enjoy watching the dances and visiting the craft exhibits.

THE NANTICOKE-LENNI LENAPE INDIAN CENTER at 18 East Commerce Street in downtown Bridgeton is the headquarters where tribal meetings are held. Indian crafts, beadwork, and dances are taught the children, and some have learned words and expressions in the Lenape dialect from recordings made by the last surviving native speakers. Craftwork is on sale at the center, and visitors are always welcome. However, these people who have faced many prejudices do not want to be looked on as curiosities; they ask only that they be treated with respect.

When we were driving back from Bridgeton I said to the boy, "Now that you have seen New Jersey Lenape descendants, what do you think?"

"They don't look like the Indians on TV," he replied. "I guess someone must make up those stories about Indians wearing war paint and scalping white people because they don't like us."

"You will have to decide about that yourself," I answered, "now that you have seen some Indians. When you go back to school on Monday you can tell the other kids how you met some real live Lenape descendants and they didn't even carry tomahawks."

As we approached the Delaware River Bridge the fading sun silhouetted the Wilmington skyline in the west, and time didn't permit visiting Raccoon and Penn's Neck to show the boy where the Swedes built the earliest Lutheran churches in New Jersey. The original churches are no longer standing, but at Raccoon (present-day Swedesboro) the Trinity Episcopal Church, erected in 1784, is near the site of the first Swedish church built in New Jersey, and the St. George Episcopal Church at Penn's Neck (present-day Churchtown near Pennsville) erected in 1811, is near where the second Swedish church stood. The historical backgrounds and the early records of both churches are discussed in a book edited by Amandus Johnson in the reading list below.

We learned during our visit to New Jersey that a number of Swedish-Americans, and other interested persons, had formed in 1983 a non-profit corporation called the New Sweden Company to memoralize the founding of the Swedish colony. We were told that one of the major projects was the construction of a seventeenth-century Swedish farmstead at Bridgeton as a permanent tourist attraction. Members of the organization intend to build an outdoor museum consisting of log structures similar to those erected by the early Scandinavian settlers. Typical residential and farm buildings will be included to give the visitor an insight into the life style of the early Scandinavians who settled in the Delaware valley. Two craftsmen specializing in early folk housing came to New Jersey from Sweden to participate in the project and to supervise and assist the members of the New Sweden Company and other volunteer workers.

When I said goodbye to my grandson after returning to Wilmington, he said, "I had a lot of fun today, Grandaddy. When are you going to take me to see some other places?"

I had a feeling that history had won hands down over television that day, and that there might even be a budding historian in the family. As time permits, I'll try to take my grandson to see some of the other places described below which might further whet his interest in history.

The following listing is not exhaustive and is not intended to be a guidebook. It is merely my personal choice of a number of places having some relevancy to New Sweden on the Delaware which the reader may want to visit.

THE OLD TOWN HALL at 512 Market Street Mall in Wilmington was built 1798–1800 as a center of social and political activities, and is now owned and maintained by the Historical Society of Delaware as a museum. Changing exhibits are devoted to Delaware history and artistic achievement. Timely displays relating to Swedish history and culture are periodically scheduled and are listed well in advance on the Society's calendar which should be consulted.

Opposite the Old Town Hall at 505 Market Street are the offices and library of the HISTORICAL SOCIETY OF DELAWARE. The library provides free and open access to a collection of books, newspapers, photographs, pamphlets, and rare manuscripts, totaling some 3 million items. References pertaining to the history of New Sweden and to the genealogy of Swedish and Finnish Americans are found in the collections.

Members of the staff will be glad to assist researchers and also to direct visitors to points of interest in the adjacent Wilmington Square and elsewhere in downtown Wilmington although these attractions may not specifically relate to the early Swedish settlement. Further information on sights to see in Wilmington can be obtained at the Mayor's office, City County Building,

800 French Street, or at the Delaware State Chamber of Commerce, One Commerce Center, Suite 200.

The Delaware State Development Office, 45 The Green, Dover 19901 will gladly supply literature and information on the numerous historical sights elsewhere in the state, some of which appertain to the early Swedes.

If limited to choose six places to visit in the Wilmington area as general tourist attractions, I would select the following, named in the order of their accessibility from downtown Wilmington:

DELAWARE ART MUSEUM   2301 Kentmere Parkway
DELAWARE MUSEUM OF NATURAL HISTORY   Kennett Pike, Greenville
HAGLEY MUSEUM AND LIBRARY   Route 141 near the intersection of Route 100
WINTERTHUR MUSEUM AND GARDENS   Route 52
LONGWOOD GARDENS   Off Route 1 north of Kennett Square

In Chester, Pennsylvania, off the Kerlin Street Exit of Route I-95, immediately opposite 1148 Concord Avenue, is a beautiful pink marble monument executed by the Finnish sculptor Wäinö Aaltonen bearing this inscription: "This Memorial erected in 1938 by the Finnish Nation and the Finns in America in commemoration of the Finnish pioneers of the first permanent settlement in the Delaware Valley in 1638."

The sculptor has depicted life-size figures in bas relief of pioneer Finnish families on the front and back of this striking monument. Two polished-stone benches on either side of the memorial are inscribed for Washington, Massachusetts, Michigan, and Minnesota. Finnish descendants in these states were responsible for this commendable effort to keep alive the memory of the role of their ancestors in New Sweden. Delaware, Pennsylvania, and New Jersey, the hearth of the Swedish-Finnish colony, are not represented in the memorial, an apparently inadvertent oversight.

On Concord Avenue near the memorial is a historical tablet

erected by the Pennsylvania Historical Commission that reads: "FINLAND—Name given to tract along Delaware River from Marcus Hook to Chester River. Grant for tract was given Captain Hans Ammundson Besk a native of Finland, by Queen Christina in 1653. Site of first Finnish settlement in America." It is correct that on August 20, 1653, Queen Christina granted land to Amundson "extending to Upland Creek," but no southern boundary was mentioned, "in consideration of his zeal and fidelity." Amundson was commander of the ill-fated *Cat*, the Swedish vessel seized by the Spaniards in the West Indies in 1649 as described in Chapter 6. Amundson was on his way to New Sweden on the *Haj's* voyage in 1654 to claim the land in America he had never seen when he died and was buried in Puerto Rico. The land was never confirmed to his heirs because of the objections of freemen who had already occupied and developed it.

At the corner of East Third and Welsh streets in Chester is "the Old Swedes Burial Ground," an unkempt cemetery overgrown with grass and weeds and crowded with old gravestones, most with illegible inscriptions. According to tradition, Armegot Printz gave this land to the Swedish church, but for that I cannot vouch. St. Paul's Episcopal Church formerly stood here, I was told, but no evidence of the church remains.

One grave has been carefully attended to—the resting place of John Morton (1725–1777), descendant of Mårten Mårtenssen (anglicized to Morton Mortonson), a Finn who accompanied Governor Rising to New Sweden in 1654. The suffix "son" was dropped by later generations. John Morton, a farmer who supplemented his income by surveying, was elected a member of the Pennsylvania Assembly and a representative to the Stamp Act Congress in 1765. He became a member of the two Continental Congresses and a signer of the Declaration of Independence. A marble obelisk nine feet high marks his grave, its four sides squared with the compass, with appropriate inscriptions on each side.

*   *   *

About seven miles north of Chester is the Governor Printz Park at Essington, administered by the Pennsylvania Historical and Museum Commission. Here on what was called Tinicum Island stood Fort New Gothenburg, Governor Printz's manse named Printzhoff, the Swedish log church, and other farm and residential dwellings built by the Scandinavian settlers. The area is no longer recognizable as an island; with stores, restaurants, and residences it appears to be part of the mainland. It should not be confused with Little Tinicum Island, a true island in the middle of the river plainly visible from Governor Printz Park.

Adjoining the park is the private property of the Corinthian Yacht Club. Archaeological work there was carried on under WPA funds in 1937 and by the Pennsylvania Historical and Museum Commission in 1976. A complex cluster of foundations were uncovered and a large quantity of colonial artifacts, such as white clay pipes, bottles, utensils, etc., as well as Indian relics. Nevertheless, the foundations of Printzhoff, the church, the fort, and the graveyard of the church have not been pinpointed with certainty because of fires, later intrusive structures, and other soil disturbances. However, markers in the park and on the Yacht Club grounds, including a small bronze tablet on the club's porch, keep alive the memories of Printz's farmstead.

On Darby Creek, two or three miles west of Governor Printz Park, is the MORTON HOMESTEAD in Prospect Park, a hewn-log residence restored and preserved by the Pennsylvania Historical Commission but at present operated by the American Swedish Historical Museum. The first section, a one-room cabin, was built by Morton Mortonson sometime after his arrival on the *Örn* with Governor Rising in 1654. About 1698 a second one-room cabin was built alongside the first with a narrow road running between them to the bank of the creek. The two structures were later connected by a central stone structure. The house was long thought to be the birthplace of John Morton, "the signer," great grandson of the original owner, but Ruth L.

Springer's research contradicts this; see her book in the reading list.

The Gloria Dei Church at Swanson Street and Delaware Avenue, east of Front Street in Philadelphia, is the successor to the log church on Tinicum Island. Actually a Swedish blockhouse built at this location ca. 1669 was converted for use as a church when the church on Tinicum Island was vacated, and it served until 1700 when the new brick sanctuary was dedicated. It became a Protestant Episcopal church in 1845, but old graves in the cemetery date back to the Lutheran congregation, the earliest dated 1708. Relics transferred from the church on Tinicum Island include a wood carving in the form of an open book surrounded by two cherubim and bearing a biblical quotation, and a stone baptismal font brought to Tinicum from Sweden. The original church bell at Tinicum was moved to the belfry at Gloria Dei, where it rang for services until the Revolution. It was recast in 1806, partially from metal in the original bell, but it still retains its original clapper.

Although New Sweden ceased to exist in 1655, the Swedish Lutheran Consistory in New Sweden continued to support Lutheran churches until 1786. These are all now Episcopal churches. In addition to those already named above, readers interested in their Swedish-Lutheran antecedents may want to visit three other Pennsylvania churches: St. James Church of Kingsessing in West Philadelphia; Christ Church of Upper Merion at Bridgeport in Montgomery County; and St. Gabriel's Church at Douglassville, Berks County.

The AMERICAN SWEDISH HISTORICAL MUSEUM at 1900 Pattison Avenue in Philadelphia aims at promoting a better understanding of "the historic and continuing influence of Swedish people on the cultural, social, economic, and political development of the United States." It is sponsored by an organization of about 1,000 members and maintains a research library comprising 13,000 volumes on Swedish-related subjects and an archival collection of letters and other manuscript material. Some of the permanent collections, and the changing exhibits, relate to New Sweden; others deal with later Swedish experience and influence on American art, music, architecture, literature, and science. The original art-work collection includes three sculptures by Carl Milles, seventy etchings by Anders Zorn, and paintings by Carl Larsson.

At 1300 Locust Street in downtown Philadelphia is the headquarters, office, library, and museum of the HISTORICAL SOCIETY OF PENNSYLVANIA. The Society owns the most extensive collection of documents, art, and museum pieces relating to the history of Pennsylvania. The manuscript depository is the largest in Pennsylvania and one of the most important in the United States. Documents relating to New Sweden are included in the collections.

The Society owns six original paintings by the Swedish-American artist Gustavus Hesselius (1682-1755) including a self-portrait, the only known likeness of the artist. Visitors are welcome to the museum, and the library's facilities are open to researchers.

Although the INDEPENDENCE NATIONAL HISTORICAL PARK in Philadelphia has nothing to do with the early Swedish settlements, no visitor should overlook INDEPENDENCE HALL, THE LIBERTY BELL, CARPENTER'S HALL, OLD CITY HALL, and other attractions related to the birth of the nation.

Three of the many other worthwhile places to visit in Philadelphia are:

FRANKLIN INSTITUTE   20th St. & Benjamin Franklin
   Parkway
PHILADELPHIA MUSEUM OF ART   25th St. & Benjamin
   Franklin Parkway
ACADEMY OF NATURAL SCIENCES   19th St. & Benjamin
   Franklin Parkway

About twenty-five miles north of Philadelphia, and within a convenient drive, is PENNSBURY MANOR (five miles east of Levittown). This site is within the bounds of the original New Sweden. The manor house William Penn lived in during his second visit to his province, 1699 to 1701, has been reconstructed and furnished with seventeenth-century antiques. The mansion and the country estate with its formal gardens and outbuildings is maintained by the Pennsylvania Historical and Museum Commission. Penn befriended the Swedish settlers, and reconfirmed to them tracts of land they were occupying in the province when he arrived in America. Several Swedes served as interpreters in Penn's meetings with the Lenape, and others were members in the earliest Pennsylvania Assembly under the Penn government.

The institutions cited above have changing time schedules, and some charge admission fees. Visitors should check by phone for information in advance of a visit to avoid disappointments.

SELECT READING LIST

Titles of books only are given. For papers and articles relating to New Sweden check the Historical Society of Delaware, the Historical Society of Pennsylvania, the Historical Society of New Jersey, or local libraries.

Acrelius, Israel. *A History of New Sweden; Or the Settlements on the the River Delaware*. Trans. William M. Reynolds. Philadelphia: Historical Society of Pennsylvania, 1874.

Biorck, Tobias Eric. *The Planting of the Swedish Church in America*. Trans. Ira Oliver Northstein. Rock Island: Augustana College Library, 1943.

Burr, Horace, trans. *The Records of Holy Trinity (Old Swedes) Church Wilmington, Del. [1697-1773]*. Papers 9. Wilmington: Historical Society of Delaware, 1890.

Clay, Jehu Curtis. *Annals of the Swedes on the Delaware*. Chicago: John Ericsson Memorial Committee, 4th ed., 1938.

Dunlap, Arthur. *Dutch and Swedish Place-Names in Delaware*. Newark: University of Delaware Press, 1956.

Eckman, Jeannette. *New Castle on the Delaware*. Wilmington: New Castle Historical Society, 3rd. ed., 1950.

————. *Crane Hook on the Delaware 1667-1669.* Wilmington: Delaware Swedish Colonial Society, 1958. Reprinted 1987.

Ferris, Benjamin. *A History of the Original Settlements on the Delaware.* Wilmington: Wilson & Heald, 1846. Reprinted by the Delaware Genealogical Society, 1987.

Gehring, Charles T. ed. and trans. *New York Historical Manuscripts: Dutch, vols. 18-19, Delaware Papers (Dutch Period).* Baltimore: Genealogical Publishing Co., Inc., 1981.

Harrington, Mark R. *The Indians of New Jersey, Dickon Among the Lenape.* New Brunswick: Rutgers University Press, 1963.

Hoffecker, Carol E. *Readings in Delaware History.* Newark: University of Delaware Press, 1973.

————. *Delaware, A Bicentennial History.* New York: W.W. Norton, 1977.

————. *Delaware, The First State.* Wilmington: Delaware Historical Commission, 1987.

Holm, Thomas Campanius. *A Short Description of the Province of New Sweden.* Trans. Peter S. Du Ponceau. Philadelphia: Memoirs of the Historical Society of Pennsylvania, 3, 1834. Illustrations of Lenape Indians in the original edition (1702) engraved by the author are imaginative and not authentic. They are omitted in this translation.

Johnson, Amandus. *The Swedish Settlements on the Delaware.* Philadelphia: Publications of the University of Pennsylvania, 1911, 2 vols.

————. *The Swedes on the Delaware 1638-1664.* Philadelphia: International Printing Co., 1927.

———. *The Instruction for Johan Printz*. Philadelphia: Swedish Colonial Society, 1930.

——— ed. *Records of the Swedish Lutheran Churches at Raccoon and Penns Neck 1713-1786*. Woodbury: Gloucester County Historical Society, reprint, 1982.

Kastrup, Allen. *The Swedish Heritage in America*. St. Paul: Swedish Council of America.

Kraft, Herbert C. *The Lenape*. Newark: New Jersey Historical Society, 1986.

Leiby, Adrian C. *The Early Dutch and Swedish Settlers of New Jersey*. Princeton: D. Van Nostrand Co., 1964.

Lindeström, Peter. *Geographia Americae*. Trans. Amandus Johnson. Philadelphia: Swedish Colonial Society, 1925.

Myers, Albert Cook, ed. *Narratives of Early Pennsylvania, West New Jersey, and Delaware*. New York: Charles Scribner's Sons, 1912.

Munroe, John A. *Colonial Delaware, A History*. Millwood: KTO Press, 1978.

Paxson, Henry D. *Where Pennsylvania History Began*. Philadelphia: George H. Buchanan Co., 1926.

Pomfret, John E. *The Province of West New Jersey 1609-1702*. Princeton: Princeton University Press, 1956.

Reed, H. Clay. *The Delaware Colony*. London: Crowell-Collier Press, 1970.

Springer, Ruth L. *John Morton in Contemporary Records*. Harrisburg: Pennsylvania Historical and Museum Commission, 1967.

Wallace, Paul A.W. *Indians of Pennsylvania*. Revised by William H. Hunter. Harrisburg: Pennsylvania Historical & Museum Commission, 1981.

Ward, Christopher. *Dutch and Swedes on the Delaware 1609-1664*. Philadelphia: University of Pennsylvania Press, 1930.

Weslager, C.A. *Dutch Explorers, Traders, and Settlers in the Delaware Valley 1609-1664*. Philadelphia: University of Pennsylvania Press, 1961.

————. *The English on the Delaware 1610-1682*. New Brunswick: Rutgers University Press, 1967.

————. *The Delaware Indians, A History*. New Brunswick: Rutgers University Press, 1972.

————. *The Log Cabin in America*. New Brunswick: Rutgers University Press, 1969.

————. *Swedes and Dutch at New Castle*. Wilmington: Middle Atlantic Press, 1987.

Wourinen, John W. *The Finns on the Delaware 1638-1655*. New York: Columbia University Press, 1938.

[author not named] *The Swedes and Finns in New Jersey*. American Guide Series. Bayonne: Jersey Printing Co., 1938.